LET MY PEOPLE GO
That They May Serve Me!
Breaking Satan's Assignments Against Your Household

Angeline L. Williams

Presented To:

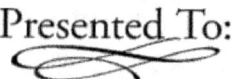

_____

From:

_____

Date:

_____

LET MY PEOPLE GO That They May Serve Me!!
Breaking Satan's Assignments
Against Your Household

Copyright © 2023 Angeline L. Williams

ISBN: 978-1-7325258-5-6

Published by Redemption Books

All rights reserved. This book or parts thereof may not be reproduced in any form, stored in a retrieval system, or transmitted in any form by any means—electronic, mechanical, photocopy, recording, or otherwise—without prior written permission of the publisher, except as provided by United States of America copyright law.

Book and Cover design by Williams DocuPrep
www.williamsdocuprep.com

Unless otherwise noted, all Scripture quotations are taken from Scripture taken from the New King James Version®. Copyright © 1982 by Thomas Nelson. Used with permission. All rights reserved.

Angeline L. Williams

Dedication

Grace and peace,

This book is dedicated to every believer who has decided to accept the mandate to tell Satan, "This is what the LORD says: Let my people go, so they can worship Me" and share the vision God has given me to reach the world for Jesus Christ in these end times. My prayer is that God will use you tremendously in the Kingdom of God to set captives free.

All my love and prayers.
God's servant,
Angeline

Contents

Dedication 1
Introduction 5
    Let us pray: 9
God Always Had a Plan 11
    Types and Shadows in Exodus 12
    Christ Is Our Moses 13
    Trouble In the Garden 15
    The Plan Begins 19
    The Next Phase 24
Spiritual Warfare 30
    Pharaoh, Not Just a Man 38
    Primary Tactics of Satan 42
        Temptation 47
        Deception 53
        Fear 54
        Unforgiveness 54
    Can A Christian Be Demon Possessed? 61
    Man's Free Will 62
    Servanthood or Slavery 64
Our Spiritual Weapons 69
    Our Spiritual Armor 69

- The Belt of Truth 70
- The Breastplate of Righteousness 71
- The Gospel of Peace 71
- Shield of Faith 71
- The Helmet of Salvation 72
- Sword of the Spirit 72
- Prayer 73
- Our Offensive Weapons 74
  - Praise And Worship 74
  - Sword of the Spirit 75
  - The Mind of Christ 76
  - Pulling and Casting Down 77
  - Binding and Loosing 77
  - The Blood of Jesus 79
  - The Name of Jesus 80
- Strongholds 81
  - Physical Strongholds 81
  - God As Our Stronghold 83
  - Incorrect Image of God 84
  - Spiritual Strongholds 87
- Ungodly (Satanic) Strongholds 89
  - Occultic Strongholds 95
  - Family Strongholds 98
  - Rejection Stronghold 106

- Stronghold of Addiction 114
- Stronghold of Fear 128

There Shall Be No Negotiations 129
- "Go, sacrifice, but stay within Egypt." 130
- "Only ye shall not go very far away." 136
- "Go you who are men." 138
- "Go, only let your flocks and herds stay." 140

Not A Hoof Shall Be Left Behind! 142

Praying In the Spirit 149
- Wield Your Sword 150
- Scriptures for Battle 160

About The Author 169

Angeline L. Williams

Introduction

"And the LORD said to Moses, "Rise early in the morning and stand before Pharaoh as he comes out to the water. Then say to him, 'Thus says the LORD: "Let My people go, that they may serve Me." —Exodus 8:20:

Everyone is having a hard time. No one is exempt, but when it's you who is going through them, it can feel like you are the only one. For several years, it seemed that I was under intense satanic attacks. I noticed that the attacks would come each time I tried to step out on faith, attempting to do what I sensed God was saying to me. My thinking was all off and not good. I was growing, and I'm still growing. I pray that I never stop growing in Christ.

There were times when I became overwhelmed and discouraged and would do things that only made things worse. The most amazing thing about it all is that I began to develop an extreme hunger for the Word of God. Even to this day, I can spend hours studying and meditating on the Word of God. I thank God for the attacks because they caused me to seek God, grow closer to Him, and strengthen my faith.

One day when I was praying, I don't remember about what, but I do remember God saying to me, "When you speak to the people and when you write, I want you to be transparent." God began to give me titles of what I thought might be sermons and books, and I would write them down, not knowing what God wanted me to do with them. I hadn't written a book since my first book of poetry when I was a teen, and I hadn't stepped into the call to preach. I've noticed that the books I've published thus far that God has given me to write have come during intense warfare and prayer and seem to be a continuation of each other. The same is true for this book. Each book so far is a book that, when studied with the Holy Spirit and the Word of God, will help saints grow in their Christian lives, as they have helped me and others who have shared their testimonies with me.

This book came about one morning when I was praying for myself, my sons, and their families. As I was praying, the Holy Spirit told me to tell Pharaoh, "Thus says the LORD: Let My people go, that they may serve Me." I thought it was something He wanted me to study, so I kept praying and made a mental note to study this passage. Then I heard the words again tell Pharaoh: *"Thus says the LORD: Let My people go, that they may serve Me."*

This time I asked, "God, do you want to declare this

over my sons or me?" Again, I heard God say to tell Pharaoh, "Thus says the LORD: Let My people go, that they may serve Me."

Over the years, I've learned that when God gives me a word, there is a lesson in it for me first, then for the people. Any preacher who preaches the true Word of God will tell you this. So I always seek God's lesson for me first. As leaders and members of the Fivefold, we have to put down the magnifying glass and pick up a mirror because sometimes the place where we need to start is within us. If we don't see ourselves correctly, how can we possibly help anyone else with their issues?

I did as I was instructed, and by faith, I called out my name and the names of my sons and declared, *"Pharaoh, thus says the LORD God: "Let _____ and _____ go, that they may serve Me."*

Apparently, that declaration had a mighty powerful effect in the spiritual realm, because it wasn't long before all hell broke loose in the house, and I was under a spiritual and physical demonic attack. Because of the severity of the attack and who Satan used to attack me, I was shocked and thrown off guard. I didn't expect what happened. I retreated to my room to pray. I had no words, and I needed the Holy Spirit to pray for me, so I prayed in tongues as I sought His guidance on what to do. As I began to calm down and the tears stopped, God began to give me understanding. He led me to the story of the Exodus of Israel, found in Exodus chapters seven through twelve. The main characters are Moses and God, and Pharaoh and Satan.

As God spoke I took notes on what He was telling me and saved them on my laptop, thinking that I would eventually do a blog post, but I realized that the notes were forming a book. Then, when I was just about done, my computer was literally destroyed, broken into pieces. This is the second book that I have been working on, and my computer was destroyed near the end. The first book was *"Put The Word in Your Mouth."*

I have received many testimonies from people who have read it—about how the revelations God gave in that book have changed their lives. When my laptop was destroyed, I realized even more of the power of the message in this book. But my computer was destroyed, along with the file with all my notes. "Holy Spirit, what do I do now?" I prayed. The Holy Spirit instructed me to take notes on my phone until God replaced my computer, so I did.

There are no words that can truly express the hurt and heaviness that entered my heart because of what was done and who it was done through. I know who was really behind the act. I know it wasn't the person who wanted to hurt me. I doubt that they even had a clue that they were being used in such a way. I have forgiven the person, and I've asked God to forgive them too and to set them free. I continue to pray and praise God for their release from Satan's grip. One thing I do know is that I will not stop praying and believing God for their freedom. I will continue to stand and declare in the name of Jesus *"Pharaoh, thus says the LORD God: "Let _____ and _____ go, that they may serve Me."* I will not compromise with Pharaoh—Satan. He will not have his way. He will let God's people go so that they may serve the Lord GOD. God has declared that it shall be so, and it will be so.

If God led you to this book, then the message within is for you. God wants you to pray for and declare His Word of deliverance over those in your life and even yourself. The assignment is to tell the stubborn spirits in your life and the lives of your family and whoever God leads you to *"Thus says the LORD: "Let My people go, that they may serve Me."*

Let us pray:

> *"Heavenly Father, as we open Your Word, I pray that You open our hearts so that we may receive revelation and understanding that will enable us to walk by faith. As the Bible says, Lord, we walk not*

by feelings or sight but by faith. Make us more effective vessels equipped for service in the Army of God to set free men and women everywhere from the bondage and enslavement of a diabolical enemy, the devil. Now to Him who is able to keep us from stumbling and present us blameless before the presence of His glory with great joy, to the only God, our Savior, through Jesus Christ our Lord, be glory, majesty, dominion, and authority, before all time and now and forever. Father, I thank You for anointing this message. Let it touch thousands of lives worldwide, equipping them for service. In Jesus' name, we pray. Amen.

Angeline L. Williams

God Always Had a Plan

Hannibal Smith, played by George Peppard in the mid-1980s television show "The A-Team," would say after every successful job they did, "I love it when a plan comes together." It is always good to have a plan. A goal without a plan is just a wish. God has always had a plan. From the very beginning, when He created the universe, God had a plan—a plan of redemption. It started long before you and I came to earth, long before the Children of Israel were delivered from the bondage of Egypt, and long before Adam and Eve sinned in the Garden of Eden. God's incredible plan of redemption began before time began. Jesus' words in His prayer before He went to the Cross, *"for You loved Me before the foundation of the world," John* 17:24 confirms this fact.

Israel's exodus not only shows God's deliverance of Israel from Pharaoh in Egypt, but it also set the stage for King Jesus to deliver His people from their sins and conquer the devil (Matthew 1:21; Colossians 2:15). Nothing just happens, and no one is here on earth or shows up in your life by happenstance. Every moment is a part of God's strategic plan. God uses ordinary people just like you and me to accomplish His will. He empowers us with supernatural gifts and the ability to do the extraordinary.

Unfortunately, as much as He has called and equipped us, He can't use some people because they have attempted to fit God into their little boxes, and many are too fearful to step out of the boat (Matthew 14:25–30). Jesus said the work He did, we will do and even greater. He gave us the tools and told us to use them to accomplish our assignment. The Holy Spirit helps us learn what those tools are and how to use them so we can impact the world for the kingdom of God.

Types and Shadows in Exodus

In the Bible, we see symbolic pictures of future events called types and shadows. The Exodus story has several types and shadows within it that hint at God's amazing plan of redemption. The original item or picture is called the type, and what it is picturing is the shadow. Types and shadows can help us see and understand God's remarkable plan more clearly. Some types and shadows in the Exodus story are:

- Israel is a "type" of God's people.
- Egypt is a "type" of the world's system which is under the control of Satan.

- The Egyptian army is a "type" of the fallen angels who followed Satan in his attempt to overthrow God in heaven.

- The children of Israel's slavery in Egypt is a "type" of slavery to sin. Israel's calling out of Egypt is a "type" of God calling us out of the world's system.

- Pharaoh chasing after the nation of Israel is a picture of how Satan pursues us after we are saved.

- The blood on the doorposts is a "type of salvation by the blood of the Lamb.

- Israel's crossing the Red Sea is a "type" of baptism. It symbolized cutting off the old way of living, leaving Egypt behind. The Bible says they "were all baptized unto Moses in the cloud and in the sea." (1 Corinthians 10:1-2)

- The children of Israel's history is a "type" of the Christian life. I'm sure you can recognize some of what they experience as children of God in your Christian walk.

Christ Is Our Moses

If there was one Bible character whose task was much like that of Christ, it was Moses. If there was ever a character in the Bible who was the most like Satan, it is the pharaoh in the Exodus story.

In John 5:39, Jesus indicated that the stories in the Old Testament were ultimately about Him. He said, *"You search the Scriptures because you think that in them you have eternal life; and it is they that bear witness about me."* As I mentioned earlier, Moses foreshadowed Jesus Christ in many ways. During the time of Moses' birth, the pharaoh ordered the mass killing of every Hebrew male child under the age of 2 years. During the time of Jesus' birth, King Herod ordered the mass killing of every Hebrew baby under the age of 2 years old.

Moses brought the Israelites out of slavery in Egypt. Jesus brought the world out of slavery to sin and death. Moses led Israel to the entrance of the Promised Land, and Jesus leads anyone who will believe and place their faith in His work on the cross to the ultimate Promised Land (reconciliation with God and eternal life), should we choose to go. Both Moses and Jesus controlled the sea. Both Moses and Jesus would go to the mountain to get instructions from God. Both Moses and Jesus gave up a life of luxury for the sake of enslaved people.

There are many other parallels between Moses and Jesus, but there is one major difference: Moses was a man (human) just like you and me who, because of his faith in God, was able to do many amazing things in the power of

God. Jesus, both human and God, lived a perfect life, showed us how to do amazing things in the power of God, and defeated sin. He says, *"Truly, truly, I say to you, whoever believes in me will also do the works that I do; and greater works than these will he do, because I am going to the Father."*

In the book of Exodus, chapter 3, God told Moses that He had heard His children's cries and He had come to deliver them. He was inviting them out of Egypt to worship Him and make sacrifices to Him. He was inviting them to come into agreement with the destiny He had for them. He was pulling them away from the surrounding nations, separating them from what was familiar so that He could set them apart for His purpose. He was inviting them to be His covenant people. He had a distinctive plan for their destiny, but this Pharaoh (Satan) stood in the way.

Trouble In the Garden

On each day of creation after completing His work, "God saw that it was good" (Genesis 1:4-25). On the sixth day, with the creation of man, God saw that it was "very good" (Genesis 1:31). People were very good. There was no sin in mankind. God created Adam and Eve in His image and His likeness. In God's eyes they were perfect and complete beings and that's how they saw themselves. God created a beautiful garden and placed them in it and told Adam to "work it and keep it." "To keep" in Hebrew is shamar," which means to guard, keep watch, keep safe, preserve, and protect. The Amplified Bible, Classic Edition version says, *"God took the man and put him in the Garden of Eden to tend and guard and keep it."*

Eden was good, but apparently it wasn't completely secure because God told Adam to "guard the garden." If God told Adam to protect the garden, there must have been something dangerous prowling around in Eden he needed to watch out for, but who or what was it? Several Scriptures lead me to believe Satan and his fallen angels lurking outside the Garden.

In Ezekial chapter 28 the Lord indicates that Satan was in the Garden of Eden: "You *were in Eden, the garden of God"* (Ezekial 28:13). Speaking to the Pharisees, He refers to Satan's deception of Eve as murder when He says: *"You belong to your father, the devil, and you want to carry out your father's desire. He was a murderer from the beginning, not holding to the truth, for there is no truth in him"* (John 8:44).

In the book of Revelation, the Apostle John identifies the serpent when he describes a future incarnation of Satan as "the great dragon": *"The great dragon was hurled down—that ancient serpent called the devil, or Satan, who leads the whole world astray"* (Revelation 12:9). So, there is no doubt in my mind that it was Satan, in the form of a serpent, who appeared, tempting Eve, and promoting what God had forbidden as good.

Man had been given the task of ruling over the animals (Genesis 1:26-28). As a ruler, Eve should have rebuked the serpent for being in open rebellion against the Lord rather than listening to the serpent. Maybe she didn't know, but surely Adam did, so when Eve brought the fruit to Adam, he should have rebuked her rather than participating in the rebellion.

Genesis 3:1 says, *"the serpent was more crafty than any of the wild animals the Lord God had made."* Undoubtably, Satan chose the serpent because craftiness and sneakiness were traits of his. He still does this today. He looks for character traits in us that he can use to his advantage. Be careful of the enemy using your weaknesses for his work. If you are prone to anger, lust, pride, or abuse of power, be careful lest the enemy use you.

Angels are spiritual beings who can function in the physical realm. Satan and demons (unclean spirits) are spiritual beings that can enter people and animals. For example, Luke 22:3 records that Satan entered Judas; and in Matthew 16:23, we read that Peter was influenced by

Satan, and many demons in Mark 5:10–13 entered the swine. So again, it's not a stretch to see that Satan used a real serpent to deceive Eve. They usually run in packs and work together to effectively torment and destroy their human victims (Luke 8:30-31, Matthew 12:43-45). The ruling spirit is often the first to enter or attack a person, usually through trauma in childhood or a generational curse.

Before the fall, Adam and Eve had perfect communion and fellowship with God. They were free, accepted, and innocent. Genesis 2:25 describes them as being naked and without shame. They didn't know they were naked. They didn't even know what naked was. After the fall, they were separated from the fellowship they enjoyed with God (Genesis 2:18). They looked at themselves, and they became more aware of their bodies and the flesh than their spirit man and they became aware of their sin. Drowning in guilt and shame, they hid themselves from God, who already knew what they had done (Genesis 3:8–10). Their actions reveal an amazing truth about God, mankind, and sin.

Sin makes people want to hide from God. The same thing that occurred in the Garden is the same thing that is going on today. Many of us have done the same as Adam and Eve and hidden from God, or like Cain, who just left the presence of God and settled elsewhere (Genesis 3:9–

10, 4:16). Generally, when life is good, and we make good choices, we rejoice with God and see this as God blessing us. However, when we make a mistake or mess up, we tend to hide and run from God instead of going to Him with it. 1 John 3:20 says, *"whenever our heart condemns us, God is greater than our heart, and He knows everything."* (ESV).

Satan has three objectives: steal, kill and destroy. You'll look up and see that he has subtly brought in all kinds of other troubles (strongholds) that lead to destruction. So whatever you think you are hiding and keeping from God, He already knows. He wants to help you face it and restore you. The correct action is to bring Him your guilt, shame, and sin, and let Him make you whole again.

God was aware of Adam and Eve's actions, and He was also the only one who could restore their relationship. What Adam and Eve did didn't surprise God at all. He had a plan in place to bring ultimate restoration for all mankind through Jesus Christ, who was slain for mankind's sin before the foundation of the world (Revelation 13:8).

The Plan Begins

Time goes by and God is ready to get things started to bring His plan of redemption into the earth. He chooses a man named Abram to be a conduit for salvation.

"Now the Lord said to Abram, "Go from your country and your kindred and your father's house to the land that I will show you. And I will make of you a great nation, and I will bless you and make your name great, so that you will be a blessing. I will bless those who bless you, and him who dishonors you I will curse, and in you all the families of the earth shall be blessed." (Genesis 12:1-3)

God told Abram (later called Abraham) to settle in Canaan. Abraham and Joseph are two of my favorite characters in the Bible, next to Jesus, and like Jesus they are key figures in God's incredible plan of redemption. Although he had faults, Abraham is primarily known for the depth of his faith. In the Book of Genesis, believing God's promise to make him the father of many nations, Abraham obeyed God's command to sacrifice his son Isaac, but God substituted a ram in Isaac's place.

The ram was a type of Jesus Christ, who would one day be sacrificed once and for all for mankind's sin. Through Abraham's loins comes Jesus Christ (the Seed), and through Christ all mankind is offered entrance into God's plan of redemption by sheer grace (Romans 5:12). The old covenant with Abraham is fulfilled through Jesus Christ.

In the New Testament, Paul explains that all Christians are Abraham's seed and therefore God's children and heirs. God later told Abraham that his descendants would become enslaved for four hundred years in the future, but He would eventually save them (Genesis 15:13). Egypt would be the land where they would become enslaved, and God had a strategic plan to get them there. Joseph, the great-grandson of Abraham, would be the next one God uses to keep in the plan of redemption. Here is how the plan unfolds:

Jacob, his father, had twelve sons. Joseph, the youngest, was favored by his father, who gave him a special coat of many colors. Joseph was having dreams, which he knew were from the Lord and revealed God's purpose and plans for his life. His brothers were jealous of him already, but their jealousy worsened when Joseph shared two of his dreams with them. In the first dream, the brothers were gathering wheat in the field, and the brothers' bundles bowed to Joseph's bundle.

In the second dream, Joseph envisioned the sun, the moon, and eleven stars (symbolizing his parents and brothers) bowing to him. These dreams foretold the future, which was all part of God's strategic plan of redemption. The brothers' jealousy came to a head, and they sold him to a caravan of traders. He was eventually brought to

Egypt, where he was sold to Potiphar, one of the pharaoh's ministers. Potiphar's wife falsely accused Joseph of coming on to her. This made her husband angry, and he sent Joseph to prison. Even in the midst of all of this, God's plan of redemption was at work.

The Lord was with Joseph during his time in prison. The jailer favored Joseph, and he was promoted to leadership. In prison, Joseph interpreted dreams for high officials. The pharaoh had two dreams, which none of his advisors were able to explain. Joseph, then thirty, interpreted the pharaoh's dreams as a divine prediction for seven years of plenty followed by seven years of famine and advised the pharaoh to prepare by storing enough grain during the first seven years to cover feeding the people during the famine. The pharaoh was so impressed by Joseph's wisdom that he appointed him his viceroy, second only to himself, and put him in charge of preparing the nation for the years of famine.

The famine came, and its effects were felt in Canaan, where Joseph's family was. Joseph's family got word that there was grain in Egypt, so Jacob sent Joseph's brothers there to buy food. Long story short, Jacob and his family moved to Egypt to both live in better conditions and be with his son Joseph. The pharaoh offered Jacob everything he needed to take care of his family in Egypt.

Joseph ruled in Egypt for 80 years until his death at the age of 110. You can read the remarkable story of Joseph in Genesis chapter 37. What amazes me most about the story is God's strategic positioning. Joseph's exile into Egypt was required for Israel's protection as a nation and the fulfillment of prophesy.

After Joseph died, Egypt was ruled by a new pharaoh who had never met Joseph. The Israelites had become so numerous that the new pharaoh feared that one day they would turn against the Egyptians. Gradually, he forced them into slavery. Even in the midst of slavery, Israel prospered. The pharaoh confined the Israelites to Goshen. The word Goshen means "approaching" or "drawing near." Despite the difficulties of being in bondage for centuries, the nation of Israel grew into a nation of millions.

Exodus chapter 1 describes the Egyptians' futile attempts to stifle the Israelites' growth. God continued to prosper them by making them more fruitful than their host nation, despite all of Pharaoh's efforts to the contrary. All of this was part of God's extraordinary plan of redemption. There is more, much more as you will see.

Joseph believed God. The dreams and visions God gave him placed an image in his heart and mind that continued to encourage Joseph to overlook the circumstances that took place in his life and operate in faith. When God wants you to pursue a specific direction for your life, He will give you a vision or a dream that will create a burning desire to work towards that goal.

The Next Phase

God was committed to upholding the promise He gave to Abraham that He would create his offspring into a great nation. The land of Goshen was very fruitful, and many of the Israelites were happy there. In fact, they began to forget their separate origins. If God had left them to themselves, they would have melted right into the Egyptian race and lost their identity as God's special people. Time goes by, and God chooses Moses to continue His plan of redemption into the earth.

Romans 15:4 says, *"For whatsoever things were written aforetime were written for our learning, that we through patience and comfort of the scriptures might have hope."* This means that the amazing true stories in the Word of God are there to teach us, to inspire us, and to help us live a godly life as we go through this life on earth. Even so, there are some stories that we tend to rush through because they are familiar to us or do not interest us at the time. The Exodus story is one such story for me. I've heard the stories of Moses, the ten plagues, the Ten Commandments, the golden calf, and the tabernacle, but until God said to declare, *"Pharaoh, thus says the LORD: Let My people go, that they may serve Me,"* I had never really studied the story.

Both actors played their roles so well that when I think of Israel's exodus from Egypt, the movie "The Ten Commandments," with Charlton Heston as Moses and Yul Brenner as Pharaoh, always comes to mind. Until God brought it to my attention, I never really paid too much attention to the pharaoh in the Exodus story. I was aware of the plagues and the miracles, but I hadn't really thought much about the pharaoh beyond the fact that he was a stubborn man who wouldn't let the nation of Israel leave, and God had to show him that He alone was the Sovereign, Almighty God.

The Bible doesn't tell us this man's name, so I always thought Pharaoh was his name. However, as I researched, I learned that "pharaoh" is a title given to the kings of Egypt over time. The word is translated as "great house," which refers to the royal palace or residence of the king and his court, similar to the White House in America.

The pharaohs were considered to be both kings and gods. The pharaoh wore a headdress comprised of snake and cobra symbols. Who else in Scripture is symbolized by a snake? That's right – Satan. Revelation 12:9 says "...that old serpent, called the Devil, and Satan." In Exodus 7:12, when Aaron's snake swallowed up Pharaoh's snakes, it was as if God was saying, "You think you are a god, but I am the only God. I can swallow you up, and when you're gone, there won't be any evidence that you ever were." This is what we want for ourselves, our family, and our friends.

The Egyptian culture worshiped a multitude of gods and goddesses whom they believed could assume the form of animals, so animals, insects, and birds were sacred to them. They believed their pharaohs were intermediaries between the many gods and humans, and they worshiped him as the incarnation of the Egyptian sun god. As I studied, I could see how the spirit that controlled this pharaoh is very prevalent in the world today. I could clearly see why God said to decree *"Pharaoh, thus says the LORD God: "Let my people go, that they may serve Me."*

Every born-again Christian has been rescued from spiritual Egypt, a place of rebellion and wickedness against God. Understand that God did not deliver you from Egypt so you can live your life your own way, on your own terms or simply for yourself. No sir, no ma'am. As Christians, we are called to be servants "of" the Kingdom of God and servants "for" the Kingdom of God. Each of us is born for a specific purpose. Great or small, we have a place and an assignment in the Kingdom of God.

One thing I can say as a mother is that most mothers know their children. Like each of us, Moses was born for a specific purpose. He was born a Hebrew slave, but he grew up in the royal palace. The story of Moses' birth and the exodus of the nation of Israel is a remarkable display of God's love, mercy, and power. Let's explore what God wants us to glean from the story. Many of us are familiar with the Exodus story, so for the sake of time and space, I will paraphrase much of it. As you study this book, when you see the word pharaoh, think Satan.

Every born-again Christian has been rescued from spiritual Egypt, a place of rebellion and wickedness against God.

Like with Joseph, there will be failures and setbacks that will try to block you from accomplishing your goals, fulfilling your God given destiny. This is how Pharaoh (Satan)operated then, and it is how Satan operates now. Like He did with Joseph, Jesus and many others, God will use your enemies to catapult you to success. No matter how many setbacks occur, instead of crumpling and complaining, find a way to serve others. Ask the Holy Spirit and He will show you what to do. Serving others is serving God.

For God is not unjust so as to overlook your work and the love that you have shown for his name in serving the saints, as you still do. —Hebrews 6:10 ESV

Therefore, my beloved brothers, be steadfast, immovable, always abounding in the work of the Lord, knowing that in the Lord your labor is not in vain. — 1 Corinthians 15:58 ESV

God will open the doors that are outside your control. He will show you how to apply specific Scriptures to your life to direct you towards His plan (Psalm 119:105). Recognize that God is with you and that you are anointed and highly favored. Serve others with all your heart. Reject the desire to murmur and complain. Praise God, thank Him for everything, and believe that God will complete what He has begun in your life.

Joseph served and ministered to the needs of others, and God blessed the work of his hands. If Joseph did it, so can you. God has promised that if you seek first His kingdom and righteousness (His will and purpose), all these things (everything you need) will be added to you. You have the same power dwelling in you that raised Jesus from the dead. You are anointed and empowered to prosper in every area of life, no matter the circumstance you find yourself in.

Scripture tells us that the devil comes to steal the

Word away (Luke 8:11-12). Trouble will come to test your character and your faith, but keep in mind who you truly are and wait on God. Joseph had extreme wealth and power at his disposal, yet he waited on the Lord in faith as He brought the dream to fulfillment! The fascinating story of Joseph is covered in Genesis, chapters 37–50. Take some time to read it with the Holy Spirit. It is an interesting story with pertinent lessons about God's sovereignty and what it means to live according to God's Word.

Spiritual Warfare

We live in a world that has two realms: a natural realm and a spiritual realm. Everything in the physical realm is either influenced by or caused by something in the spiritual realm. Behind every issue we face is a spiritual root. You might not be able to see all the activity going on behind the scenes, but you certainly feel the effects. Just like physical people occupy the natural realm, God and His holy angels and the devil and his demons (fallen angels) occupy the spiritual realm.

In the New Testament, notably Paul's writings, the language of spiritual warfare is pretty constant. Scripture tells us that in the spiritual world, there is continuous warfare being waged between good and evil, between Satan and God, and between the devil and man. It all started in the Garden of Eden.

> *2 Kings 6:15-17: "15 When the servant of the man of God rose early in the morning and went out, behold, an army with horses and chariots was all around the city. And the servant said, "Alas, my master! What shall we do?" 16 He said, "Do not be afraid, for those who are with us are more than*

those who are with them." ¹⁷ Then Elisha prayed and said, "O Lord, please open his eyes that he may see." So the Lord opened the eyes of the young man, and he saw, and behold, the mountain was full of horses and chariots of fire all around Elisha." (ESV)

Colossians 3:1-3: "¹ Since, then, you have been raised with Christ, set your hearts on things above, where Christ is, seated at the right hand of God. ² Set your minds on things above, not on earthly things. 3 For you died, and your life is now hidden with Christ in God." (NIV)

Also read Colossians 2:13-15.

When I first got saved, several books in the Old Testament seemed violent to me. Moses was fighting wars. Joshua and David were fighting wars, Sodom and Gomorrah were destroyed, this all seemed violent. David even says in Psalm 18:34 and in Psalm 144:1 that God trains his hands for battle, his fingers for war. As I matured, the Holy Spirit revealed what was really happening during this time. I began to see that much of it, including the exodus of Israel, was a time of intense spiritual warfare.

Although the conflict between God and Satan, Moses and Pharaoh, Israel, and Egypt was played out on earth, it was a spiritual battle. The ten plagues on the pharaoh were a spiritual conflict between God and the spiritual powers of evil controlling the pharaoh and the Egyptian people. The battle with Satan's magicians Janees and Jambres, the victory of God over the gods of Egypt through the plagues, and the miraculous deliverance at the Red Sea, all show God's great power over Satan and his forces.

The nation of Israel was escaping a nation that worshiped idols and was filled with evil spirits. They passed through nations that were full of evil spirits. God protected His people during the plagues in Egypt, delivered them, and provided for them when they left Egypt and through each nation that they traveled through. God wanted His people to be free of all evil spirits, and He wanted them to learn to fight their battles in His strength and by His Word. This is still what He wants for us today. He may not always prevent the battles we have with Satan, but He always gives us victory through them.

As uncomfortable as it may be to think about, the Bible also makes it very clear that mankind is involved in this ongoing spiritual warfare. In the spiritual battle, God and Jesus try to draw people to the kingdom of light and righteousness through faith in Jesus Christ. Satan and his demonic forces constantly try to steal the hearts of people away from God and hold them in his kingdom of darkness.

In the book of Revelation, the Apostle John wrote that

in the end times, there will be an increase in demonic activity. I hear people complaining, saying, "The devil sho is busy," as they go on a rampage discussing the problems going on in their lives. Unless you are in a deep spiritual slumber, you can see that there is some force of darkness at work in our world today. Satan is running rampant in this hour. We see wars, violence, lives destroyed by drugs, human trafficking, the destruction of family life, and the list goes on and on. Confusion is everywhere you look.

My heart breaks when I see so many of our young people with no respect for their lives or the lives of others—robbing, killing, selling drugs, gang banging, and ending up spending their lives in prison. There is an epidemic in the land of family estrangement, and specifically close to my heart are adult children estranged from their parents. There is identity confusion everywhere you turn. It's not just a person's confusion about how God created them, but saints of God who don't know their identity in Christ. Many saints constantly question their salvation and see trials as a sign that God has abandoned them. They forget that they have the Holy Spirit in them. They live with their past hanging over their heads and accept spiritual bondage and affliction as a normal part of the Christian walk.

Satan has several weapons that he uses in his attempt to cause us to fall. I believe that deception is his primary weapon. Do not underestimate Satan's power to deceive. He is not called the "Father of Lies" for nothing (John 8:44). In the movie, "The Usual Suspects," there is a quote by Roger "Verbal" Kint, played by Kevin Spacey, that says, "The greatest trick the devil ever pulled was convincing the world he didn't exist." This is truly Satan's greatest trick. I believe this is true. His second greatest trick is convincing the church that we blame too much on the devil. I don't believe we blame him enough.

It doesn't matter what destructive behavior a person might be involved in, whether it is drugs, alcohol, lust, self-condemnation, guilt, depression, or any other destructive behavior, Satan is behind it. Satan is very clever. He has been on his mission of destruction for centuries. Satan may use people and strategies to persecute us. He may use people to lie to us, cheat us, hurt us, or even kill us! Satan, our real enemy, is behind it. So when someone hurts us, it can be hard to grasp that the actual attack comes from something we can't see rather than from the person or circumstance right there in our face. But think about this. We can't see the wind. But we can certainly feel it. And if we are in the midst of a tornado or hurricane, we can certainly feel its effects. As long as we see people as enemies and wrestle with them, we are fighting the wrong enemy.

Many people, even Christians, don't realize the

spiritual significance or the warfare that is taking place in their lives. They forget that Satan is involved, or they view things as only natural or physical. Some say when we were redeemed we are immune to demonic activity. It is clear from the many examples of Jesus and the apostles lives, as well as several passages of Scripture, that this is a lie.

Some have convinced themselves that we should not get involved in spiritual warfare and deliverance because it is not biblical or because they have an unhealthy fear of demonic power. Some say they believe the Bible is true, yet they don't pay much attention to what most of it says. They believe much of it is not relevant to us today, and to some, God's Word often seems impossible to live by. Many have heard that we are in a spiritual battle, but they haven't seriously reckoned with this truth or put forth the effort to learn how to function effectively in the battle.

The early church understood how active demonic powers were in the world. God warns us in Hosea 4:6 that we, His people, are destroyed for lack of knowledge because we reject His knowledge. People don't realize how much their lack of knowledge contributes to Satan's goal to destroy them. If God wants us to lay down and do nothing to fight against the spiritual attacks we constantly face, which Paul describes as spiritual warfare, then why has He given us the tools to bring victory in this area? And why would Paul warn us to make sure we aren't ignorant of Satan's devices? (2 Corinthians 2:5–11).

Jesus gave His church power over all evil. Nowhere in Scripture do we see it being withdrawn. Our failure to conquer evil is not because we don't have the power, but rather because of unbelief, ignorance, and negligence (Matthew 17:14–18). There are many examples in Scripture showing that Satan and his hosts suffered total defeat because of Christ's followers exercised faith in Jesus' name. This can and should be the experience of the church today.

Whether you believe in spiritual warfare and deliverance or not, regardless of how much you may want to ignore it as a believer in Christ, you have been enlisted in a war against Satan and the forces of darkness. You are in a battle that will last until you leave this earth. The attacks we experience will come in varying degrees. Some may seem like little skirmishes. Some might seem never ending and some may seem like an all-out war.

The more we learn the truths concerning spiritual warfare, the more prepared you will be to fight and to be victorious. With the Word of God and the help of the Holy Spirit, I want to help you understand spiritual warfare, so you will know how to effectively use the tools God has given the Body of Christ to defeat the assaults of the enemy.

The Bible warns us in 1 Timothy 4:1-3, *"Now the Spirit expressly says that in latter times some will depart from the faith, giving heed to deceiving spirits and doctrines of demons, speaking lies in hypocrisy, having their own conscience seared with a hot iron, forbidding to marry, and commanding to abstain from foods which God created to be received with thanksgiving by those who believe and know the truth."*

This is why we see such rampant growth of the occult and Satanism in our world today. In 2 Corinthians 4:4, we are told, *"The god of this age has blinded the minds of unbelievers, so that they cannot see the light of the gospel that displays the glory of Christ, who is the image of God."* Who has blinded the minds of unbelievers? Satan.

Consider the unbelievers that you know—those you encounter at work or on the street who have little to no knowledge of the gospel, although it is readily available everywhere we turn—and you wonder how they could not believe in God or Jesus Christ. Satan has blinded their minds so that they cannot see the light of the gospel. This is Satan's strategy in the lives of those who have not trusted in Jesus' sacrifice on the cross, and it is also his strategy in the lives of those who have.

His goal is to confuse, frustrate, mar the image of God, and steal the truth of God's Word that has been deposited in our lives. Another strategy Satan uses that works very well for him is to mask his activities to make it appear that someone or something else is to blame. This way we focus on and wrestle with the people, circumstances, and hindrances instead of the "real source," the Devil.

Jesus never dealt with surface problems or applied bandages. He always went straight to the source of the issue. You may be dealing with people in your life who are knowingly or unknowingly trying to block the destiny God has for you and them. No matter what you call them, anyone or anything that tries to block you or hold you down when God wants to lift you up is being used by the devil. I don't care what you call them or who they are; the devil is behind it.

Elijah called him Ahab, Shadrach, Meshach, and Abednego called him Nebuchadnezzar; Daniel called him King Darius; the Jews called him Herod; and Jesus called him Satan. Whatever or whoever stands in the way of God's children serving Him becomes God's enemy. No one in their right mind wants to be God's enemy!

Pharaoh, Not Just a Man

The spirits that controlled this pharaoh were spiritual strongholds. The pharaoh of Moses' time was a proud and brutal dictator. His power depended on his control over his subjects. He saw how the Israelites were multiplying and he was afraid they would revolt against him, so he enslaved the children of Israel and forced them to build his treasure cities, Pithom, and Raamses. When he heard that a deliverer would be born who would free the Jews, he ordered that all the firstborn male babies of the Israelites be killed. He ordered the Israelite midwives to cast every newborn male into the Nile River (Exodus 1:22).

When God sent Moses and Aaron to the pharaoh with the message, "Let My people go, that they may serve Me," he would not listen to God's messengers or heed His judgments. Letting the Israelites go would have been against his own interests. And because of his pride, he caused a great deal of pain for himself and his people, and yet, to the very end, this stubborn man refused to repent and let the Israelites go. Of course, Satan was behind this act.

Pride is a very serious problem that many people don't realize they have because the arrogance in their hearts deceives them. Scripture teaches that pride will destroy us, and the judgement of God will come upon those who are proud unless we humble ourselves and repent.

- *"When pride comes, then comes shame; but with the humble is wisdom." — Proverbs 11:2*
- *"By pride comes nothing but strife, but with the well-*

advised is wisdom." — Proverbs 13:10

- *"The LORD will destroy the house of the proud: but he will establish the border of the widow." — Proverbs 15:25*

- *"Everyone proud in heart is an abomination to the Lord; though they join forces, none will go unpunished.." — Proverbs 16:5*

- *"Pride goes before destruction, and a haughty spirit before a fall." — Proverbs 16:18*

- *"A haughty look, a proud heart, and the plowing of the wicked are sin.." — Proverbs 21:4*

- *"A man's pride will bring him low, but the humble in spirit will retain honor." — Proverbs 29:23*

- *"The arrogant one will stumble and fall with no one to raise him up; and I will set fire to his cities, and it will devour all his environs." — Jeremiah 50:32*

Prideful people often think more highly of themselves than they ought to. A prideful person wants their SELF to be praised, to get glory, to be worshiped, and to be highly talked about. They do not appreciate and understand God. They perceive they have no need for Him, and they do not appreciate others, so they don't relate to others well.

If you identify any pride in your heart and find yourself making it more about self and less about God, the first step is to humble yourself, then submit to God, and resist the devil! If a loved one that you are standing and praying for is being controlled by a spirit of pride, you can pray that they will humble themselves and submit to God so that God can deliver them from the spirit of pride.

Like many people today, this pharaoh may not have realized just how much he was being used by Satan to destroy his own life and the lives of others. He thought he was in charge. Satan didn't realize that he was being used by God either. The Scriptures reveal that while Satan was using this pharaoh to oppose God and frustrate His plan, God used his efforts to further His plan.

This pharaoh was the perfect example of a carnal-minded person. Romans 8:7 says, *"The mind governed by the flesh is hostile to God; it does not submit to God's law, nor can it do so."* This verse, unfortunately, describes the major spiritual problem that many people, both saved and unsaved, face. Like this pharaoh, some people will not repent until something drastic happens, and some not even then.

Primary Tactics of Satan

In Matthew chapter 13, Jesus exposes a tactic of the enemy and teaches a kingdom principle in the parable of the Sower. Many of the people Jesus is talking to are farmers, so He uses the illustration of the seed so they will understand what He is talking about. When Jesus describes what happens to the seed, He's describing what happens to it in real life. Take some time to read the entire chapter on your own, but for now, let's look at verses 37-40:

> *"37 He answered and said to them: "He who sows the good seed is the Son of Man. 38 The field is the world, the good seeds are the sons of the kingdom, but the tares are the sons of the wicked one.*
>
> *39 The enemy who sowed them is the devil, the harvest is the end of the age, and the reapers are the angels. 40 Therefore as the tares are gathered and burned in the fire, so it will be at the end of this age."*

Jesus says the Son of Man is the farmer who plants good seed. The field is the world, and the good seed represents the people of the Kingdom (the Body of Christ). The tares (weeds) are people who belong to the evil one. The enemy who planted the weeds among the wheat is the devil. The harvest is the end of the world, and the harvesters are the angels. It's difficult to differentiate between the weeds and the wheat because, before the wheat produces fruit, they look identical to one another, which is why we need the wisdom of the Holy Spirit and the Word of God. The difference between wheat and tares is that wheat provides nutrients, whereas tares do not. The tares look like wheat, but they are there to destroy the wheat. Satan is not trying to look different; he's trying to blend in so that we don't even recognize that he's there. He comes as a wolf in sheep's clothing and masquerades as an angel of light to confuse people and get them to fall into his trap. God is not a God of confusion (1 Corinthians 14:33).

The only way that you won't have confusion about who is who and what is lie and truth is by reading the Word of God. This is where the leading of the Holy Spirit and discernment (wisdom) comes in because you need to clearly see who is here to oppose God and who is here to uplift God. Especially if you're searching online to get an understanding of something that God has said or is doing in your life. So many people look godly, act godly, and sound godly, but they only have the form of godliness. They are basically actors playing a part. You need the Holy Spirit and His discernment (wisdom). The Holy Spirit will always bring you the truth about whatever the situation is or whoever the person is. He will never lead you astray.

I have noticed that a lot of people who attend church

do not find their identity in Jesus Christ but rather in a church denomination, the church name, or a certain creed. They attend church every Sunday, but they are not learning or hearing what they need, and that's affecting their walk. The devil doesn't mind if you go to church. There are many who, like the Pharisee, think that dressing in their Sunday best and being visibly active at church makes them righteous and holy. Remember Jesus said, *"Not everyone who says to Me, 'Lord, Lord,' shall enter the kingdom of heaven, but he who does the will of My Father in heaven. Many will say to Me in that day, 'Lord, Lord, have we not prophesied in Your name, cast out demons in Your name, and done many wonders in Your name?' And then I will declare to them, 'I never knew you; depart from Me, you who practice lawlessness!'"* (Matthew 7:21-23).

Remember, the enemy cannot control you unless you give him access. Certain environments will grow certain things. Certain fruits and vegetables will only grow in certain climates and environments. What I am saying to you is to be careful what you listen to, the places you frequent, and who you hang around with. My mother used to say, "Association brings on assimilation. You are the company you keep, so be careful of who you surround yourself with." What she was conveying to us was to be careful who you hang around with because if they are doing things they shouldn't be doing, you could very well end up participating in the activities.

> *Association brings on assimilation. You are the company you keep, so be careful who you listen to, and who you surround yourself with.*

Proverbs 13:20 says it like this: *"He who walks with wise men will be wise, but the companion of fools will be destroyed."* You might be headstrong and prideful and say, "Well, it won't affect me in the same way," but what you are doing is giving a foothold to the enemy to start planting different weeds, so you are growing wheat now."

What is the foothold? Imagine you're trying to close the door to your home, and someone sticks their foot in the door to keep it from closing, and you walk away thinking that the door is closed, but it's not. This is an example of giving the devil a foothold.

Looking at things from a fleshly standpoint, you cannot tell the difference between wheat and tare. Just like a farmer would have to be knowledgeable about what seeds produce, you need to know the seeds that the enemy comes to plant and how he does it. We'll go over some of them here. But you are going to need to get with the Holy Spirit and study the Word of God.

In 2 Corinthians 11:4, Paul talks about a group of people who were preaching another Jesus and another gospel. Some people were doing the same thing in Galatia. To the Believers there, Paul said,

> *"¹ O foolish Galatians! Who has bewitched you that you should not obey the truth, before whose eyes Jesus Christ was clearly portrayed among you as crucified? ² This only I want to learn from you: Did you receive the Spirit by the works of the law, or by the hearing of faith? ³ Are you so foolish? Having begun in the Spirit, are you now being made perfect by the flesh?"*

People in the Body of Christ who are bought and paid for by the blood of Jesus are smudging (burning sage), spraying ammonia around their home and their church building to ward off demons, and performing other fleshly things to ward off evil spirits, ignoring the power of God within them. Because they still go to church every Sunday and give their tithes and offerings, they think everything is okay, but it is not! O foolish Galatians! How have you allowed the ways of the world to replace the Word and power of God? Jesus expelled demons by His word.

The Word of God tells you not to lean on your own understanding, but to seek His will in all of your ways, and He will show you which path to take (Proverbs 3:5-6).

Listen to what God says, don't be deceived. Take the time to learn the nature of God and His Word for yourself. Jesus tells us in John 10:10 that Satan's overall agenda is to "steal, kill, and destroy." There are various ways that he and his demons accomplish this. Just as God is strategic in His plan, so is Satan. Just as God has a plan for your life, Satan has one, too.

Satan despises you and has a terrible plan for your life. If he cannot deprive you of eternal life, he will consistently try to prevent you from experiencing the benefits of serving God in this life. Since Satan cannot be in more than one place at a time, he delegates demons (principalities, powers, rulers of the darkness, and spiritual wickedness in high places) who distract, discourage, divert, and deceive through a variety of tactics and strategies. So let's talk about a few of the more common tactics of demons so you can better understand and recognize their agenda.

Temptation

Temptation does not disappear when you become a Christian. Your flesh is not saved, which is why Paul says you must bring it under subjection to the Word of God (1 Corinthians 9:27). You still have the same desires you had before; you have to diligently apply the principles of the Word and build up self-control to defeat these. Although the enemy is very busy in our lives and is behind everything that pulls us away from the things of God, we cannot pass the buck and responsibility for our sin onto the enemy.

> *"13 Let no one say when he is tempted, "I am tempted by God"; for God cannot be tempted by evil, nor does He Himself tempt anyone. 14 But each one is tempted when he is drawn away by his own desires and enticed. 15 Then, when desire has conceived, it gives birth to sin; and sin, when it is full-grown, brings forth death." —James 1:13-15*

The Lord will test us, but He doesn't tempt us. Temptation comes when there is something you desire in your heart that is not of God. Its agenda is to get you to fall into something that is against your God-given destiny. Therefore, it is important to recognize, know, and understand what temptation is and where it comes from. If we begin to see everything as demonic, we will begin to believe that we have no personal accountability or responsibility for our own sin and our actions.

The Lord doesn't test us because He doesn't know what's in us. He tests us because He wants to reveal to us what's in us. The Bible says God cannot be tempted by evil, nor does He tempt anyone. But each person is tempted when they are drawn or dragged away by their own evil desire. These evil desires are the lusts of the flesh. The Scripture above says that after desire has been conceived or we come into agreement with it, it gives birth to sin. And sin, when it is fully grown, brings forth death. This Scripture shows the stages of temptation. In 1 Corinthians 10:13 Paul says:

> "No temptation has overtaken you except such as is common to man; but God is faithful, who will not allow you to be tempted beyond what you are able, but with the temptation will also make the way of escape, that you may be able to bear it."

Look at the mercy of God. He will not let you be tempted beyond what you can bear. He will always give you a way out.

The Lord doesn't test us because He doesn't know what's in us. He tests us because He wants to reveal to us what's in us.

When you have an urge to do any of these things, recognize that you don't have to do them (Romans 6:11–13). Find the exit, then run like something dangerous is chasing you, because it is. Meditate on the fruit of the Spirit in Galatians 5:22–23, which are love, joy, peace, longsuffering, kindness, goodness, faithfulness, gentleness, and self-control. Against such, there is no law. Also remember,

Jesus told His disciples (us!) to pray, *"Lead us not into temptation, but deliver us from evil,"* so pray that you are not led into temptation.

Now if you give your authority and your will over to your flesh, it will rule you. If you give yourself over to the ways of God and commune with and listen to the Holy Spirit, if you are committed to pursuing the things of God, you will step into His grace—His divine empowerment to overcome. So there is no type of temptation that you will ever encounter that there is not enough grace for you to overcome. But you must be connected and stay connected to the source of grace.

So, if you're wondering if the temptation you're facing is your flesh or demonic, in Galatians 5:19–21, Paul gives us a partial list of the works of the flesh:

> *"19 Now the works of the flesh are evident, which are: adultery, fornication, uncleanness, lewdness, 20 idolatry, sorcery, hatred, contentions, jealousies, outbursts of wrath, selfish ambitions, dissensions, heresies, 21 envy, murders, drunkenness, revelries, and the like; of which I tell you beforehand, just as I also told you in time past, that those who practice such things will not inherit the kingdom of God."* (NKJV)

In 2 Timothy 3:2, Paul gives an extensive list of

attributes found in evil people in the last days.

> "2 People will be lovers of themselves, lovers of money, boastful, proud, abusive, disobedient to their parents, ungrateful, unholy, 3 without love, unforgiving, slanderous, without self-control, brutal, not lovers of the good, 4 treacherous, rash, conceited, lovers of pleasure rather than lovers of God— 5 having a form of godliness but denying its power. Have nothing to do with such people." —2 Timothy 3:2-5 (NIV)

Notice that we see all these things in both passages going on all around us today. Maybe the temptations you deal with are not on these two lists, but whatever they are, they are no different from what others experience.

Listen to what the Word of God says and you won't be deceived. Take the time to spend time with God and study His Word for yourself.

Also consider how impressionable we are. Have you ever changed your mind because of something someone said to you? Whether you would like to admit it or not, our lives have been influenced by other people's suggestions. Satan is a master of the power of suggestion. He has been using it since the Garden of Eden. Because there are limits to what he can do to us, the enemy will use the power of suggestion to plant negative, discouraging seeds in your mind to get you to sin.

> *If you give your authority and your will over to your flesh, it will rule you.*

All temptation is rooted in deception. Many people have suffered for years because someone has placed negative thoughts about them in their minds. They believe it, and they continue to water and fertilize that seed by rehearsing it over and over in their minds, and it grows into a huge, bitter tree. Then they have to deal with the damaging results. Or maybe we planted something intentionally or unintentionally in someone's mind. It is in your mind where you will lose or win the battle. Keep in mind that Satan and his demons lurk around, studying you, waiting for the opportunity to devour you. He knows your desires, so he won't present you with something that you don't desire.

Judas' greed made him ripe to be tempted by Satan. Jesus warned Peter that Satan desired him and prayed for him, but Peter basically said, "No need; I got you." Then, Jesus prophesied that he would deny Him three times that day (Luke 22:31–34). Satan tempted Ananias (Acts 5:1–11). Of course, he was still responsible for his actions. All three of them had demonic activity working in their lives—

demonic temptation.

Satan even went after Jesus trying to tempt Him towards sin and trick Him out of His destiny. Since Jesus was not born of a man, he did not have a sinful nature, so he couldn't be tempted by sin. Apparently, Satan knew this, but he tried Jesus anyway. With his suggestions, Satan was trying to put thoughts into Jesus' mind, as he did with Eve in Genesis Chapter 3. Jesus had been fasting for 40 days and was hungry. His physical body may have been a little weak, so Satan tried to take advantage of His weakness. If Satan tried Jesus, he will certainly try you.

Deception

We've talked about how the devil uses deception as a key weapon against people. Remember, John 8:44 says Satan is the father of all lies. Satan will deceive anyone who will listen to him. He tries to convince people that the Bible is outdated and that people who believe it lack understanding of reality. He lies about God. He deceives us about who we are, about who God is, what God has called us to do. He uses the desires in our corrupt human nature, our flesh to deceive us. Deception is not always easy to recognize.

Fear

Fear is another powerful demonic strategy that Satan uses against us. The Bible instructs us to fear (reverence) the Lord and respect Him. Fear is another one of Satan's counterfeits. He wants people to fear and revere him. But the fear he brings is a fear of terror. Fear is Satan's strategy against faith. Fear kills our faith. Again, Satan goes after our minds. Fear strikes our minds. Faith stems from the heart. Demons want you to be afraid of them and will use fear to paralyze us—to cause us to fear death, fear them, fear life, and basically just live in fear. 2 Timothy 1:7 says, *"God has not given us a spirit of fear, but of power, of love, and of a sound mind."*

If you are praying for someone (especially for deliverance and salvation), you may find yourself under demonic attack. The person may seem to get worse, and if the person has a demon, it may manifest and act out through the person, all to try to intimidate you and cause you to fear them and stop praying. This is Satan trying to get you to stop praying. Don't stop!

Unforgiveness

Many people give the enemy access in their lives without knowing it through unforgiveness, unhealed hurts and wounds. Unforgiveness is a sin. Sin makes our hearts fertile ground for Satan's seeds of lies to be planted. Unforgiveness is toxic to the soul. It is one of the most powerful enemies in the body of Christ. Many illnesses and infirmities are directly related to unforgiveness. Forgiveness has the power to heal you. Many people have been healed instantly once unforgiveness has been released.

Unforgiveness is most often committed against those we're closest to. Husbands won't forgive their wives; wives won't forgive their husbands; children won't forgive their parents, and parents won't forgive their children; Christians who will not talk to each other and cannot even look at each other; pastors who will not forgive church members; and believers who will not forgive their pastor.

Forgiveness is not saying what a person did to hurt you is okay. It hurt, and it wasn't okay. You might feel anger. It's okay to feel anger, but it's not okay to stay there. Holding onto anger creates a bitter root and gives the enemy a foothold in your life, and he will string you around like a puppet. Also, this stronghold will lie to you and make you believe that not forgiving the person who hurt you gives you some type of power over them, especially if they want to be forgiven. The truth is that not forgiving them gives unforgiveness power over you. As long as we choose not to forgive anyone for any offense, you basically choose to have a shackle attached to your ankles.

Forgiveness is not forgetting what happened, but rather acknowledging that God decided to pardon your offender—as well as all of us—on the day that He sent His son Jesus to die. Once we realize how much we have been forgiven, it becomes much easier for us to forgive others. Scripture tells us to *"forgive as the Lord forgave you"* (Colossians 3:13).

I'm not saying that forgiveness is always easy, but what I am saying is that it is a choice. One that we all have. If God can forgive, so can we. When the pain is still there, the thought of extending forgiveness to the person who hurt us might be the last thing on our minds and the hardest thing to do. Depending on the offense, forgiveness may be a process that you will need to strive towards. If something is keeping you from being forgiving, such as bitterness, sadness, or humiliation, you may need to keep asking the Holy Spirit to help you tear down the stronghold while erecting a fortress of compassion in its stead. Forgiveness is not optional.

Giving and receiving forgiveness are two sides of the same coin, it is a double-edged sword. In the parable of the unforgiving servant in Matthew 18:21-35 Jesus described what would happen should we choose not to forgive:

"²¹ Then Peter came to Him and said, "Lord, how often shall my brother sin against me, and I forgive him? Up to seven times?" ²² Jesus said to him, "I do not say to you, up to seven times, but up to seventy times seven. ²³ Therefore the kingdom of heaven is like a certain king who wanted to settle accounts with his servants.

²⁴ And when he had begun to settle accounts, one was brought to him who owed him ten thousand talents. ²⁵ But as he was not able to pay, his master commanded that he be sold, with his wife and children and all that he had, and that payment be made. ²⁶ The servant therefore fell down before him, saying, 'Master, have patience with me, and I will pay you all.' ²⁷ Then the master of that servant was moved with compassion, released him, and forgave him the debt.

²⁸ "But that servant went out and found one of his fellow servants who owed him a hundred denarii; and he laid hands on him and took him by the throat, saying, 'Pay me what you owe!' ²⁹ So his fellow servant fell down at his feet and begged him, saying, 'Have patience with me, and I will pay you all.' ³⁰ And he would not, but went and threw him into prison till he should pay the debt.

³¹ So when his fellow servants saw what had been done, they were very grieved, and came and told their master all that had been done. ³² Then his master, after he had called him, said to him, 'You wicked servant! I forgave you all that debt because you begged me. ³³ Should you not also have had compassion on your fellow servant, just as I had pity on you?'

³⁴ And his master was angry, and delivered him to the torturers until he should pay all that was due to him. ³⁵ "So My heavenly Father also will do to you if each of you, from his heart, does not forgive his brother his trespasses." (Matthew 18:21-35 NKJV).

Peter is curious as to whether it is acceptable for him to maintain resentment or seek retribution after forgiving someone seven times. Can the person exact revenge without incurring God's wrath if, after seven times, they continue to harm others?

Seven times is not enough, Jesus warns Peter. God demands "seventy times seven" forgiveness from him. Peter must be like, What?" Seven times seven, times seven, is 490 times. I don't think that's what Jesus was trying to say to Peter, though. In the Bible, the number seven represents completion, and perfection. When Jesus said, "Seventy times seven," He was saying, "Peter, you must continue to forgive to perfection and completion." You must keep forgiving until the offense has healed.

There was an incident that happened in my life when I had to literally pray every waking hour for almost a year, asking God to help me forgive the person. I was finally able to release the pain. I think this is what Jesus meant. In the parable, the servant's master was angry, and he delivered him to the torturers until he should pay all that was due to him. Jesus says, *"This is what My heavenly Father will do to you if you do not forgive others their trespasses."* For all the trouble unforgiveness causes, it is just not worth it! Jesus taught us to pray, *"Forgive us our debts, as we forgive our debtors"* (Matthew 6:12).

Spiritual warfare is much more than binding and casting out demons in Jesus' name. Spiritual warfare is forgiving those who hurt or persecute you, blessing them, and trusting God to avenge you. Without forgiveness, it's impossible to have a relationship with God.

Jesus said, *"Whenever you stand praying if you have anything against anyone, forgive him, that your Father in heaven may also forgive you your trespasses."* (Mark 11:25) So unforgiveness will hinder your prayer life.

Forgiveness is a weapon, a powerful one that is often

neglected in our binding and loosing exercises. Before you engage in combat, keep in mind that the Lord is merciful, gracious, and slow to wrath. He also abounds in mercy and lovingkindness and is tolerant of sin and transgression. (Numbers 14:18).

The power of forgiveness can be used to not only destroy strongholds, but also to keep the enemy from ever building one. Unforgiveness puts you at a disadvantage in the spiritual world. If you are imprisoned by unforgiveness yourself can you effectively bind demons?

Also, forgiveness is worship. We cannot worship God without forgiveness. Forgiveness is God's greatest work, evident in Jesus' sacrifice at the cross. The Lord is a warrior. He has never lost a fight and He never will. You can't lose if you follow His example and extend forgiveness; if you decide to fight evil with good; and if you let God exact justice.

Prayer to Break Unforgiveness Stronghold

Father, thank You for loving me, forgiving me, and saving me. I realize that I have held unforgiveness in my heart, and I want to let go of it. I ask that You forgive me for harboring ill feelings concerning my offender, and I ask that You forgive them for hurting me. Father, right now I release all anger, bad feelings, and resentment I have held towards anyone before You. I lay it all at Your feet, and I release and forgive those who have wronged me. Father, if I have held unforgiveness and anger towards You, I ask You to forgive me. Father, I know that offenses will come. Help me to make forgiveness a way of life. In Jesus' name, I pray. Amen.

Can A Christian Be Demon Possessed?

In the Bible, we see Jesus casting out demons (Matthew 8:28–9:1; Mark 5:1–21; Luke 8:26–40) and in the book of Acts we read where the Apostles cast out of demons (Acts 8). However, none of these passages indicate that those who were delivered were Christians. Christ defeated Satan at the cross, and the believer today is to live a spiritual life based on that finished victory. As Christians, we have been crucified with Christ; it is no longer us who live, but Christ lives in us; and the life which we now live in the flesh I live by faith in the Son of God, who loved me and gave Himself for me.

1 John 4:4 reads, "You are of God, my little children, and have overcome them: because greater is He that is in you than he that is in the world." Jesus, by way of the Holy Spirit, who indwells believers, is greater than the one (Satan) who is in the world. Christians have been bought and

paid for by the precious blood of Jesus (1 Corinthians 7:23). We cannot be owned by both Jesus and Satan. This is not to say that Christians will not be affected, harassed, afflicted, or influenced by a demon, but again, a Christian cannot be owned by a demon.

Think about this. If a person takes a lot of drugs or alcohol into their body, is the person under the influence of that substance or owned by the substance? The person is not owned by the substance but is under its influence. Even if they are addicted or an alcoholic, they are not owned by the substance, but the substance influences their behaviors and beliefs. For instance, say you went shopping and left the back door to your home open. When you come home, there is a thief in your house. The thief has invaded your home, but does he own it? No, you are the owner. It is my prayer that as you study this book with the Holy Spirit and your Bible, you will walk away with a deeper and more stable understanding of God's Word on the matter.

Man's Free Will

Satan is very crafty and does everything he can to keep people bound by his evils. There are people who have been taught that praying or interceding for others without their permission is asking God to manipulate someone and interfere with their free will, which is essentially witchcraft. For example, say a parent is praying for their adult child's deliverance and salvation, but the child doesn't know it, or a wife recruits a prayer group to pray for her husband to break free from some issues he is dealing with without his permission. Is the parent or prayer group praying against these people's free will? According to Scripture, no.

The Apostle Paul says in 1 Timothy 2:1-2, *"1 First of all, then, I urge that supplications, prayers, intercessions, and thanksgivings be made for all people, 2 for kings and all who are in high positions, that we may lead a peaceful and quiet life, godly and dignified in every way." (ESV)*

In Romans 8:26–27 he says, *"In the same way, the Spirit helps us in our weakness. We do not know what we ought to pray for, but the Spirit himself intercedes for us through wordless groans. And he who searches our hearts knows the mind of the Spirit, because the Spirit intercedes for God's people in accordance with the will of God."* (NIV)

Many lost people are confused and don't even know what is good for them, and God wants you to pray for them. That's what intercessors do. God gives them people to pray for, and they follow God's lead and pray for them. When you are obedient, you'll be amazed at how God will teach you how to pray specific and personal prayers, not just for others but for yourself. They don't even need to know that you or others are praying for them, but Scripture says that when you pray in secret, God will reward you openly (Matthew 6:6-7).

Servanthood or Slavery

There is a difference between "servanthood" and "slavery." God created man with free will (free will is in the soul). Adam exercised his free will when he ate from the tree. Our soul is the part of us that determines and makes decisions on our behalf. It is with our soul that we choose, accept, or reject things, ideas, and beliefs. Being a servant is a choice we make. You choose to become a servant to the Most High, God doesn't force Himself on you. You offer yourself. Unless the soul yields its rule to the Spirit, the Spirit cannot rule. You authorize the Spirit to rule when you choose to let it. This is why we have to say "yes" to salvation.

Learning to trust God to do what He said He would do is such a relief.

Being a slave to sin is a choice you make also. If you choose sin, recognize that it will never satisfy you. Sin begets more sin until it becomes so ordinary that, after a while, the thrill is gone, and you begin to search to find something a little more thrilling. And the cycle repeats itself, and before you know it, you are on a road in the wilderness, feeling like you cannot find a way out and break free. This is slavery!

Romans 6:16-18 in the New Living Translation reads, *"16 Don't you realize that you become the slave of whatever you choose to obey? You can be a slave to sin, which leads to death, or you can choose to obey God, which leads to righteous living. 17 Thank God! Once you were slaves of sin, but now you wholeheartedly obey this teaching we have given you. 18 Now you are free from your slavery to sin, and you have become slaves to righteous living."*

In Colossians chapter 3 we learn that we must put to death whatever belongs to that old earthly nature, or we are going to have a problem. Ephesians 4:22-24 says something similar: *"that you put off, concerning your former conduct, the old man which grows corrupt according to the deceitful lusts, and be renewed in the spirit of your mind, and that you put on the new man which was created according to God, in true righteousness and holiness."*

Colossians 3:5-9 gives us a list of the things that we are to put off:

"⁵ Therefore put to death your members which are on the earth: fornication, uncleanness, passion, evil desire, and covetousness, which is idolatry. ⁶ Because of these things the wrath of God is coming upon the sons of disobedience, ⁷ in which you yourselves once walked when you lived in them. ⁸ But now you yourselves are to put off all these: anger, wrath, malice, blasphemy, filthy language out of your mouth. ⁹ Do not lie to one another, since you have put off the old man with his deeds, ¹⁰ and have put on the new man who is renewed in knowledge according to the image of Him who created him," — Colossians 3:5-9

Most of us know how powerful our minds are. However, what many of us don't realize is how much our thoughts govern our lives. The thoughts that pass through our minds can influence and control our behavior, our attitudes, and our actions. Notice that Paul says in Ephesians 4:23 *"Be renewed in the spirit of your mind."*

In Romans 12:2, he says, *"And do not be conformed to this world, but be transformed by the renewing of your mind, that you may prove what is that good and acceptable, and perfect will of God."*

Paul is not suggesting that we renew our minds. Paul commands us to renew our minds because our beliefs and the things we set our minds on are key parts of how we live our lives. Because our old nature—that corrupt, sinful, fleshly nature did not automatically disappear when we got saved, we need to change our way of thinking. The old man is used to believing, talking, and acting on things that are contrary to the mind of Christ. Most of the time, we don't even realize it's leading us to a place we don't want to be until we've landed on the doorstep.

When your thoughts are not in line with the Word of God but with the world, you will speak, act, and walk according to your carnal mind.

Your mind is the area where Satan will try to get a foothold to set up a stronghold. What we choose to allow into our minds and take into our bodies will determine who controls us. Colossians 3:2 tells us to set our thoughts and affections on things above instead of on earthly things. Why? Because so often, our minds are consumed with anxiety, and worry, which causes us to stress about the things of this world that Christ has already taken care of.

When your thoughts are not in line with the Word of God but with the world, you will continue to speak, act, and walk according to what your carnal mind is telling you to do. Remember, the carnal mind is an enemy of God and stops the work of the Holy Spirit. If you want to walk in the Spirit, you will need to renew your mind. Renewing your mind means replacing your thoughts, your belief system, and Satan's lies with the truth of God's Word. It is not hard to do, but it does require faith, and faith is acting on the Word of God.

> *Being a slave to sin is a choice.*

The first step is to acknowledge that the old man, your old mind, has been crucified, and you now have the mind of Christ that you must develop. Then you want to ask God to help you transform your mind (Philippians 4:8), which He is happy to do. Then put forth the effort to fill your mind with and meditate on the Word of God daily or as often as you can (Joshua 1:8). As you take these steps, your faith will increase, and you will begin to see a transformation in your thinking. Before you know it, you will be able to set your mind on things above and live in a way that pleases God.

Angeline L. Williams

Our Spiritual Weapons

We have some powerful weapons at our disposal to use to stand up and fight on behalf of ourselves, our family, and anyone else God wants us to proclaim liberty to and over. Our weapons for this warfare are found in the truth of God's Word. They are mighty and have the power to overthrow and destroy every stronghold that has been built up through wrong believing.

Our spiritual weapons can be classified into two categories: offensive and defensive. Defensive warfare involves guarding yourself against the tactics or schemes of the devil. Offensive warfare involves tearing down the strongholds that the enemy has formed in your mind through deception and accusations.

Our Spiritual Armor

Paul describes the spiritual armor Christians can take up against spiritual enemies in Ephesians 6:11–17.

> *"[11] Put on the full armor of God so that you can stand against the schemes of the devil. [12] For our struggle is not against flesh and blood, but against the rulers, against the authorities, against the*

cosmic powers of this darkness, against evil, spiritual forces in the heavens. ⁱ³ For this reason take up the full armor of God, so that you may be able to resist in the evil day, and having prepared everything, to take your stand. ¹⁴ Stand, therefore, with truth like a belt around your waist, righteousness like armor on your chest, ¹⁵ and your feet sandaled with readiness for the gospel of peace. ¹⁶ In every situation take up the shield of faith with which you can extinguish all the flaming arrows of the evil one. ¹⁷ Take the helmet of salvation and the sword of the Spirit—which is the word of God. ¹⁸ Pray at all times in the Spirit with every prayer and request, and stay alert with all perseverance and intercession for all the saints." — Ephesians 6:10-18

The Belt of Truth

The truth exposes lies. sound teaching and a good understanding of God's truth counters Satan's deceit. The Holy Spirit is called the Spirit of truth (John 14:17; 15:26). The truth comes from God. The Holy Spirit not only helps us see the truth of God, He dwells within us and helps us to expose the truth to those whose eyes and minds are darkened by the wickedness of this world (Ephesians 4:18).

The Breastplate of Righteousness

Satan is the accuser of the brethren. He accuses us of our sins and faults before God. The breastplate of righteousness is a powerful defense against the lies of the enemy, the accusations of people around you, and any declaration. Having the assurance that we are righteous in God's sight will counter Satan's accusations.

The Gospel of Peace

The word "gospel" means good news. The good news is that Jesus has come to set the captives free from sin and give them access to Him. This is a powerful message that we bring to the world. We must be prepared for the battle. The gospel of peace helps us stand firm against the enemies of God, be bold, and share the gospel with others. You do not have to be a super evangelist; you just need to allow the Holy Spirit to show you the door to speak about Jesus and give your testimony. The Holy Spirit will do the rest. As believers, we are filled with the peace of God. Ask God to help you bring peace in a time of chaos and war.

Shield of Faith

Again, the "shield of faith", is typically held in the left hand for defense. Paul says take up "the shield of faith, with which you can extinguish all the flaming darts of the evil one" (Ephesians 6:16). Picture yourself raising a protective shield to block the fiery darts sent towards you by the enemy. The strength of the shield is not in the shield, but the faith we've placed in Christ is what makes it strong enough to extinguish all the flaming darts of the evil one."

The Helmet of Salvation

A helmet protects a soldier against damaging and deadly blows to the head. The soldier's helmet also protected his eyes, enabling him to see danger clearly. The helmet of salvation protects Believers from the devil's attacks on the mind and from the "cares of this world" that bombard our thoughts and feelings.

In 1 Thessalonians 5:8, Paul appeals to us to wear the helmet—the hope of salvation as the confidence of our salvation (NLT). With confidence in our salvation, we can trust that our salvation and all that it includes—forgiveness of sins, freedom from sin, healing, deliverance, power, authority over demons, adoption, justification, and everything else that pertains to life and godliness is secure.

Sword of the Spirit

The Word of God is one of the most powerful weapons we have to use against the enemy. It is a weapon that can be used both defensively and offensively. The enemy's greatest weapon is man's ignorance of God's Word. Hebrews 4:12 says, The Word of God is alive and active. Sharper than any double-edged sword, it penetrates even to dividing soul and spirit, joints, and marrow; it judges the thoughts and attitudes of the heart. It is important to remember that the enemy also knows the Word of God. He can quote Scripture, like he did with Jesus in Matthew 4:3-6.

God's Word can protect us from the lies of the enemy; it can also counter attack. Offensively, it can be used to claim territory for the Lord by sharing the gospel message and setting the captive free. God says in Joshua 1:8, *"This Book of the Law shall not depart from your mouth, but you shall meditate on it day and night, so that you may be careful to do according to all that is written in it. For then you will make your way prosperous, and then you will have good success."*

Prayer

Paul instructs the church to always pray in the Spirit with all supplication and prayer while pleading for all the saints. We must remain vigilant and persistent in our prayer life (Ephesians 6:18–19). We should never undervalue or give up on the power of prayer. Prayer connects us to the power of God, which is necessary to defeat spiritual enemies, so we cannot let prayer slip through the cracks.

With so much going on in the world and so many things competing for our time, we need to stay alert and be persistent in our prayers for all believers everywhere. While we may not be literally praying every waking second, there is never a good time to set prayer aside. It's a tool we need to have in constant use (1 Thessalonians 5:17). As children of God, we can boldly go to the throne of God through Jesus Christ, our Lord, and ask for help in our spiritual battles with the enemy.

Our Offensive Weapons

Praise And Worship

Praise and worship (singing, dancing, praying, being thankful for God's blessings, and declaring God's Word and Good News) create an intimate space between you and the Lord, allowing Him to speak directly to your heart and draw you nearer to Him and into your life and situations. Praise and worship are powerful weapons. There are many examples and Scriptures in the Bible of the great power of praise and worship. Two stories that particularly encourage me are found in 2 Chronicles chapter 20 and Acts 16:23-26. In 2 Chronicles 20, when Israel faced a mighty enemy, they began to sing and praise God, and God set an ambush to defeat their army. Praise was Jehoshaphat's weapon.

The other passage is Acts 16:23–26, when after Paul and Silas were thrown into prison, they praised God, and their praise caused a great earthquake, which miraculously shook all the prison doors open and everyone's chains were loosed. The Bible says in Psalms 22:3 that God inhabits the praises of His people. So God "dwells" in the atmosphere of His praise. Praise was Paul and Silas's weapon. When you offer praise and worship to God, you are setting ambushments in the spirit world.

Sword of the Spirit

The Word of God is one of the most powerful weapons we have to use against the enemy. It is a weapon that can be used both defensively and offensively. The enemy's greatest weapon is man's ignorance of God's Word. Hebrews 4:12 says, The Word of God is alive and active. Sharper than any double-edged sword, it penetrates even to dividing soul and spirit, joints and marrow; it judges the thoughts and attitudes of the heart. It is important to remember that the enemy also knows the Word of God. He can quote Scripture, like he did with Jesus in Matthew 4:3-6.

God's Word can protect us from the lies of the enemy; it can also counter attack. Offensively, it can be used to claim territory for the Lord by sharing the gospel message and setting the captive free. God says in Joshua 1:8, "This Book of the Law shall not depart from your mouth, but you shall meditate on it day and night, so that you may be careful to do according to all that is written in it. For then you will make your way prosperous, and then you will have good success." Paul said, "Take the sword of the Spirit" and declare war. Isaiah 59:19 AMPC says, *"When the enemy shall come in like a flood, the Spirit of the Lord will lift up a standard against him and put him to flight [for He will come like a rushing stream which the breath of the Lord drives]"*. The Word of God is our standard—our only standard.

The Mind of Christ

Philippians 2:5 says, *"Let this mind be in you, which was also in Christ Jesus."* The mind of Christ is not just a way of thinking. It is an anointed mind with anointed thoughts, anointed ideas, principles, and values. It is an attitude of knowing who you are in Christ and what you can accomplish through Christ. It is anointed wisdom and knowledge to know exactly how to accomplish things, when to accomplish things, and where to do it. 1 Peter 4:1 says, *"Therefore, since Christ suffered for us in the flesh, arm yourselves also with the same mind, for he who has suffered in the flesh has ceased from sin,"* The mind of Christ spiritually discerns the Holy Spirit's guidance. Ask the Holy Spirit to help you put on the mind of Christ and receive the mind of Christ by grace through faith. Take time every day to meditate on (study, rehearse, ponder and confess) the living Word of God.

Pulling and Casting Down

Paul said in 2 Corinthians 10:4, *"For the weapons of our warfare are not carnal but mighty in God for pulling down strongholds."* Our fight is not physical, but spiritual therefore we must fight in the Spirit and not in the flesh. Take every thought captive to obey Christ and fight against anything that opposes God. When you pull down and cast out Satan's strongholds, you are waging offensive warfare.

Binding and Loosing

Jesus said in Matthew 16:19, *"And I will give unto thee the keys of the kingdom of heaven: and whatsoever thou shalt bind on earth shall be bound in heaven: and whatsoever thou shalt loose on earth shall be loosed in heaven."* Bind in Greek is deo {deh'-o} meaning to bind, to fasten with chains, to throw into chains, to put under obligation, to undo, to dissolve, to forbid, to prohibit, to loose what is compacted or built together, to declare to be illicit, to annul, to subvert, to do away with, to deprive of authority, to declare unlawful, to break up, to demolish, destroy, to overthrow, to do away with.

An example of Jesus doing this is found in Isaiah 61:1, which says, *"The Spirit of the Lord God is upon me; because the Lord hath anointed me to preach good tidings unto the meek; he hath sent me to bind up the brokenhearted, to proclaim liberty to the captives, and the opening of the prison to them that are bound."*

Understand that part of your assignment is to heal those whom Satan has tried to destroy. Understand that your authority to bind is not only against evil spirits, but also for healing those whose lives have been broken apart. Jesus said, *"Heal the sick, cleanse the lepers, raise the dead, cast out devils; freely ye have received, freely give"* (Matthew 10:8). Now, let me say this: you do not have to be in their presence. He sent His word, healed them, and delivered them out of their destructions (Psalm 107:20).

To loose means to release, to untie, to set free, to unwrap, to take off.

In Luke chapter 13, Jesus gives us an example of binding and loosing. Scripture says there was a woman who had been bound by a spirit of infirmity for eighteen years. When Jesus saw her, he called her forward and said to her, *"Woman, thou art loosed from thine infirmity."* Then He put His hands on her, and immediately she straightened up and praised God (Luke 13:10-13). You have the power to bind the forces of evil and loose the forces of good.

The Blood of Jesus

When Jesus died on the cross of Calvary, He loosed us from the dominion of sin and the power of the enemy. The blood of Jesus is one of the most potent weapons against spiritual wickedness in high places and to demolish every stronghold of satanic forces. The blood of Jesus can never lose its power because it is divine blood.

Hebrews 12:24 says, *"The blood of Jesus speaks better things than the blood of Abel."* The blood of Abel cried out to God (Genesis 4:10). Abel's blood cried out for vengeance on the murderer. The blood of Jesus, on the other hand, cries out for mercy on sinners. The blood of Jesus intercedes. Revelation 12:11 says, *"They* (believers) *overcame him* (Satan) *by the blood of the Lamb* (Jesus Christ).*"*

When you testify or give evidence of the power of God in your life, you wage offensive spiritual warfare. Just as a lawyer in court bases his arguments on the law of the land, to be effective, your testimony must be based upon the testimony of the Word of God.

The Name of Jesus

The name of Jesus is not just a phrase we say at the end of our prayers. It is a powerful offensive weapon. It is a symbol of the authority and power He has given us. Proverbs 18:10 tells us that *"The name of the Lord is a strong tower; the righteous run to it and are safe."*

Joel 2:32 tells us *"Whosoever shall call on the name of the LORD, shall be delivered."* Romans 10:13 tells us, *"Whosoever shall call upon the name of the Lord shall be saved."* From the bible references above, there is a need for us to take action, either to run into that name or to call on the name.

Notice that in each of the verses there is something that we must do: run into the name of the LORD or call on the name of the LORD. Many people neglect this important fact, expecting God to do it for them. However, God acts when we obey His instructions. So when the enemy comes, ask God for instructions, follow them, and run into the name of the Lord or call on Him.

Angeline L. Williams

Strongholds

Can Christians have demonic strongholds? The dictionary describes a stronghold as a well-fortified place or fortress and as a place that serves as the center of a group, as of militants or of persons holding a controversial viewpoint. Strongholds are demonically inspired, but they are mentally and emotionally received and acted upon. Incorrect beliefs, negative emotions, addictive behaviors, etc. that have accumulated can act as a stronghold. A stronghold can develop a life of its own in a person. A stronghold can cause a person to be stuck in a rut of depression, have recurring unbelief, or have a consistent bad temper.

In the Bible there are three types of strongholds mentioned. Each time it can be defined as a fortress or hold:

1. Physical strongholds,
2. God as our stronghold, and
3. Spiritual strongholds.

Physical Strongholds

In the Old Testament, many large towns had a fortress wall surrounding them for protection. Some of them had walls so wide that chariots could run on them. These physical strongholds gave the people hope and a sense of security (Judges 6, 1 Samuel 23:14). Depending on where the spiritual stronghold has been built, it can have a significantly different purpose. For example, when the Lord becomes our stronghold, a spiritual stronghold can be a source of protection for Christians. Psalm 94:22, says: *"But the LORD has become my stronghold, and my God the rock of my refuge."*

This Scripture presents God as a safe and secure haven and a shield from the enemy.

"1 The Lord is my light and my salvation; whom shall I fear? The Lord is the stronghold of my life; of whom shall I be afraid? 2 When evildoers assail me to eat up my flesh, my adversaries, and foes, it is they who stumble and fall. 3 Though an army encamp against me, my heart shall not fear; though war arise against me, yet I will be confident." — *Psalm 27:1-3*

When King Saul was chasing David to kill him, he took refuge in a place known as "the strongholds of En Gedi." This was a desolate place, with caves built into the sides of the cliffs that were perfect for hiding. water. It was there that David penned several passages found in the book of Psalms. It was here that David came to realize that the very place that felt so isolated had become God's protection during the years of his enemy's pursuit. During those days of isolation, God provided everything David needed, even a nourishing spring in the middle of the barrenness.

God As Our Stronghold

In Psalm chapter 18, David wrote: *"¹ I love you, O Lord, my strength. ² The Lord is my rock and my fortress and my deliverer, my God, my rock, in whom I take refuge, my shield, and the horn of my salvation, my stronghold. ³ I call upon the Lord, who is worthy to be praised, and I am saved from my enemies."*

Nahum 1:7 says, *"The Lord is good, a stronghold in the day of trouble; and He knows those who trust in Him."* David calls God his stronghold for good reason. It's good to know that they can retreat within the walls of the fortress of God and abide under the shadow of the Almighty. It is comforting to know that God is my stronghold, that He is a hiding place from all the negatives that life brings.

I feel safe and secure, knowing that I can run to the Lord and find safety. I believe that when God says that He will never leave me, forsake me, or deceive me, He means it and will honor His word. It took me some time to come to this realization, but I praise God I have. To learn that I could trust God to do what He said He would do is such a relief.

The Word of God says in Numbers 23:19: *"God is not a man, that He should lie, nor a son of man, that He should repent. Has He said, and will He not do? Or has He spoken, and will He not make it good?"* Hebrews 6:18 says: *"it is impossible for God to lie."*

Incorrect Image of God

One of the most devastating strongholds a person can have is an incorrect image of who God is and how He sees us. If a person sees God as a cruel, distant, uncaring, and hard taskmaster (sort of like the pharaoh in Exodus chapters 7 through 12), they will live their lives with an unhealthy fear of God. This type of fear is not reverence or profound respect and love for God, but a fear that He is looking to pounce and punish you for every mistake or wrong thought. It makes a person paranoid and prevents them from drawing close to Him.

The fear of God is a theme that runs throughout the Bible. Unfortunately, many people have been taught to be afraid of God by people who have a religious view of God rather than a personal relationship with Him. They have a misunderstanding of what it means to fear God. Then there are those who say we shouldn't fear God because God is love, and perfect love casts out all fear. While it is true that God is love and that perfect love casts out all fear, we can't ignore that the Bible does tell us to fear God.

> *God is a Waymaker, Satan is a troublemaker. "Whoever fears the Lord has a secure fortress, and for their children it will be a refuge"*

What does it mean to "fear" God? Since there is a difference between the fear of the Lord and the terror of Him, what type of fear does God want us to have? The Bible makes it clear that to love, honor, and obey God, we must fear Him. A healthy fear of God is not the fear of consequences, but a desire to not dishonor or displease God. It causes one to draw closer to Christ. An unhealthy fear of God would be the opposite. It would bring constant anxiety and fear of torture or even punishment. No one should live this way. We live best when we live with a healthy fear of God.

In the book of Proverbs, King Solomon instructs his son on how to live a godly life. He says, *"The fear of the Lord is the beginning of knowledge, but fools despise wisdom and instruction"* (Proverbs 1:7 NKJV). He says, *"The *fear of the Lord is the beginning of wisdom, and the knowledge of the Holy One is understanding"* (Proverbs 9:10). Then he says, "The fear of the Lord prolongs days, but the years of the wicked will be shortened" (Proverbs 10:27).

In Proverbs 14:26, he says, *"Whoever fears the Lord has a secure fortress, and for their children it will be a refuge"* (NIV). I like what Oswald Chambers said about the fear of the Lord. He said, "The remarkable thing about fearing God is that, when you fear God, you fear nothing else; whereas, if you do not fear God, you fear everything else." Believers have no reason to be scared of Him. However, I pray that all unbelievers fear the judgment of God and eternal death, and give their lives to Christ.

> *"26 For if we go on sinning deliberately after receiving the knowledge of the truth, there no longer remains a sacrifice for sins, 27 but a fearful expectation of judgment, and a fury of fire that will consume the adversaries. 28 Anyone who has set aside the law of Moses dies without mercy on the evidence of two or three witnesses. 29 How much worse punishment, do you think, will be deserved by the one who has trampled underfoot the Son of God, and has profaned the blood of the covenant by which he was sanctified, and has outraged the Spirit of*

grace? ³⁰ *For we know him who said, "Vengeance is mine; I will repay." And again, "The Lord will judge his people."* ³¹ *It is a fearful thing to fall into the hands of the living God."* —Hebrews 10:26-31 ESV

Spiritual Strongholds

Spiritual strongholds can be godly strongholds or ungodly, satanic strongholds. A satanic stronghold is a tool that Satan uses to block people from God and His love. He uses strongholds to trap people into thinking, feeling, and behaving in ways that destroy their destinies. In ancient times, when the king got word that his town was coming under attack, he would send out a message for the people to retreat to the fortress and prepare for the oncoming attack. The people would run for safety inside the fortress.

God wants us to turn to Him in the same way. He wants to be our defense, our stronghold, and our protector. There is no one who can deliver like Jesus. All we need to do is believe in the finished work of Jesus. One of my favorite passages of Scripture is Psalm 91, which talks about God as a stronghold. Let's look at the blessings of God being our stronghold:

"¹ He that dwelleth in the secret place of the Most High shall abide under the shadow of the Almighty.

2 I will say of the Lord, "*He is my refuge and my fortress; my God, in Him will I trust.*" *3 Surely He shall deliver thee from the snare of the fowler and from the noisome pestilence. 4 He shall cover thee with His feathers, and under His wings shalt thou trust; His truth shall be thy shield and buckler. 5 Thou shalt not be afraid of the terror by night, nor of the arrow that flieth by day, 6 nor of the pestilence that walketh in darkness, nor of the destruction that layeth waste at noonday. 7 A thousand shall fall at thy side, and ten thousand at thy right hand, but it shall not come nigh thee. 8 Only with thine eyes shalt thou behold and see the reward of the wicked.*

9 Because thou hast made the Lord, who is my refuge, even the Most High, thy habitation, 10 there shall no evil befall thee, neither shall any plague come nigh thy dwelling. 11 For He shall give His angels charge over thee to keep thee in all thy ways. 12 They shall bear thee up in their hands, lest thou dash thy foot against a stone. 13 Thou shalt tread upon the lion and adder; the young lion and the dragon shalt thou trample underfoot.

14 "*Because he hath set his love upon Me, therefore will I deliver him; I will set him on high, because he hath known My name. 15 He shall call upon Me, and I will answer him; I will be with him in trouble, I will deliver him and honor him. ¹⁶ With long life will I satisfy him, and show him My salvation."* — Psalm 91 (KJ21)

Ungodly (Satanic) Strongholds

An ungodly stronghold will keep a person from hearing the good news from receiving the truth of their need for Christ, repenting of sin, and experiencing salvation and receiving deliverance. A person may hear a message from a pulpit or a friend about God's love. They almost hear the truth sent by the Holy Spirit to set them free, but it just bounces off the walls of a stronghold of rejection, fear, or whatever lie is holding them captive. And another voice whispers a string of lies, excuses, and thoughts that block the truth.

Most of our troubles in life are because of ungodly strongholds in our imaginations. Paul talks about strongholds when he responds to the people in the Corinth church who claimed that his letters were weighty and strong, but in person he was weak, and his speech was of no account. Basically, they were gossiping about Paul, trying to turn people away from him. This slander came from people who measured and compared themselves against each other. So naturally, they were troubled or jealous of Paul. The Message Bible tells the account like this:

"¹⁻² And now a personal but most urgent matter; I write in the gentle but firm spirit of Christ. I hear that I'm being painted as cringing and wishy-washy when I'm with you, but harsh and demanding when at a safe distance writing letters. Please don't force me to take a hard line when I'm present with you. Don't think that I'll hesitate a single minute to stand up to those who say I'm an unprincipled opportunist. Then they'll have to eat their words.

³⁻⁶ The world is unprincipled. It's dog-eat-dog out there! The world doesn't fight fair. But we don't live or fight our battles that way—never have and never will. The tools of our trade aren't for marketing or manipulation, but they are for demolishing that entire massively corrupt culture. We use our powerful God-tools for smashing warped philosophies, tearing down barriers erected against the truth of God, fitting every loose thought and emotion and impulse into the structure of life shaped by Christ. Our tools are ready at hand for clearing the ground of every obstruction and building lives of obedience into maturity.

⁷⁻⁸ You stare and stare at the obvious, but you can't see the forest for the trees. If you're looking for a clear example of someone on Christ's side, why do you so quickly cut me out? Believe me, I am quite sure of my standing with Christ. You may think I overstate the authority he gave me, but I'm not backing off. Every bit of my commitment is for the purpose of building you up, after all, not tearing you down.

9-11 And what's this talk about me bullying you with my letters? "His letters are brawny and potent, but in person he's a weakling and mumbles when he talks." Such talk won't survive scrutiny. What we write when away, we do when present. We're the exact same people, absent or present, in letter or in person." —2 Corinthians 10:7-11

Paul knew they had no understanding of the truth (2 Corinthians 10:12), so he didn't argue with them, but stood his ground. He stayed focused on his call from Christ and explained to the Corinthian church that his battle, as well as the battle of the church, was a spiritual battle that must be fought with spiritual weapons. This is a great example of how Satan will try us and how we are to respond.

I am reminded of a time in my early walk with Christ when I was going through intense warfare. I struggled as a single parent and me and my three children moved a lot.

Rumors and speculations were being spread about me in the church I attended as to why. It was a very painful time. The rumors and speculations hurt so much because they came from people whom I loved and considered brethren in Christ. God used this time to teach me about Satan, spiritual warfare, and the power of His Word in my mouth. It all led to me publishing my first book, *"Put The Word In Your Mouth."*

Gossip is a sin that many Christians get caught up in. Satan, the accuser of the brethren, is a slanderer, and he uses people to do his bidding. Maybe Satan has used or is using people to try to destroy your character. Knowing who you are in Christ, and what you have in Christ, is the key to overcoming the attack and staying on course with God's plan and purpose. Mediate on and declare God's truth (Joshua 1:8). The only way to know God's Word is to read and study it, meditate on it, and apply it to your life every day. We have powerful weapons that, when applied, will destroy false arguments and strongholds. This is what God taught me and what Paul understood.

Just because a person has strongholds that need to be dealt with does not mean they are evil or demon-possessed. Ungodly strongholds are not evil spirits, they are lies we have accepted as truth. Every person, no matter what their economic status or background, Christian or not, has ungodly strongholds in their life that need to be demolished. They are built up over time brick by brick in our mind. The process is so gradual that many times the person is not even aware it has occurred. An ungodly stronghold may be occupied by a demon or unoccupied.

Satan uses satanic strongholds to block people from God and His love.

Remember, Ephesians 4:27 warns, *"Do not give the devil a foothold."* If the lies go unchallenged by the truth of God's Word, strongholds are built, and before you know it, you are responding to the spirit's voice, believing it is your own voice. A good example of this is when an addict or alcoholic defends their substance or alcohol abuse. If Satan and his demons can convince you that sin is acceptable, or justifiable, it will be easier to get you to yield to it. For example:

- You know that the Bible says that sexual attraction to the same sex is a sin, but the sin has convinced you that you were born this way, so it must be okay.

- You think talking to a woman at work that you are physically attracted about your problems is not a problem even though she kissed you and touched you inappropriately a few times and you got excited, but you haven't had relations with her.

- You really want to be used by God, but you've done so much in the past that you think God couldn't possibly use you.

Can you see from these examples how sin can become a stronghold? Ungodly strongholds usually form from traumatic experiences or unhealed wounds. Satan usually starts forming strongholds in our minds when we are young because when we are young and vulnerable because our hearts are fertile ground for the enemy to plant lies. Some are formed because of willful sin. The devil knows that if he can kill something in its infancy, he won't have to deal with it in its maturity. He goes after young people, even starting in the womb. We'll talk more about this later. Some are learned from your environment or personal experiences, and some are generational. Some are formed through occult activities which the Bible describes as an abomination.

Below I've listed some of the more common strongholds that Satan uses to trap people today. Ask God to help you see and comprehend if any of these strongholds and beliefs might be an issue of yours. Then ask Him to help you break free.

Occultic Strongholds

"10 There shall not be found among you anyone who makes his son or his daughter pass through the fire, or one who practices witchcraft, or a soothsayer, or one who interprets omens, or a sorcerer, 11 or one who conjures spells, or a medium, or a spiritist, or one who calls up the dead. 12 For all who do these things are an abomination to the Lord, and because of these abominations the Lord your God drives them out from before you." — Deuteronomy 18:10–12

Many people, especially young people, fall prey to the evils of the occult world out of curiosity, and some are looking for power. They tamper with occult things, practice New Age and spiritualism, consult psychics and astrology, and indulge in magic, divination, sorcery, and witchcraft, all of which God warns against in the Bible, not realizing the danger ahead. They see it as a beneficial, harmless spiritual practice for entertainment, a family tradition, self-knowledge, personal or spiritual growth, healing, enlightenment, etc. And before they know it, they have become chained by evil spirits and are experiencing confusion, oppression, and much more. Breaking the hold these powers have on your life and your family is crucial.

Many have broken free of these evil spirits and shared

stories of opposition and threatening voices from the spirit realm trying to prevent them from repenting and renouncing the involvement of this evil. No matter what Satan does, Jesus has defeated him. Jesus is the Deliverer, and He will protect you.

Occult practices have been around for centuries, but today this evil is accepted as the norm. Every time you take part in any form of occult practice, you open entry points for demons to enter your life, oppress you, and lead you into deeper bondage on all levels—mental, physical, emotional, and spiritual. There is so much that can be said about the occult, but what I want you to understand is that occultic practices offend our holy God so much that He likens our involvement with the occult to "whoring with lovers." Occult practices put us under the direct influence of demons and curses. This is definitely something that you don't want to dabble in.

If you're not sure if you've dabbled in the occult, here's a brief list of some of the most popular occult practices we can come across today:

Divination: Seeking to foresee or foretell future events or discover hidden knowledge by interpreting omens or through psychic readings, witchcraft, Ouija boards, New Age and spiritualism, para-psychology (psychic phenomena), and several other occult activities. God warns in Jeremiah 27:9, *"do not listen to your prophets, your diviners, your dreamers, your fortune-tellers, or your sorcerers..."*

Astrology: Study of the planets as having an influence on human affairs and the natural world. Examples: Horoscopes, zodiac signs, consulting the lunar calendar, moon, sun or star worship, worship of heavenly bodies as deities etc. God warns in *Deuteronomy 4:19, "And beware lest you raise your eyes to heaven, and when you see the sun and the moon and the stars, all the host of heaven, you be drawn away and bow down to them and serve them, things that the LORD your God has allotted to all the peoples under the whole heaven." (ESV)*

Necromancy: Baker's Evangelical Dictionary of Biblical Theology defines necromancy as a form of divination in which a person calls upon the dead to receive communication that clarifies knowledge; communicating with the "dead" to foretell future events or discover hidden knowledge, and to bring someone back from the dead. Examples: ancestor worship, talking to dead people or relatives as a ritual, grave sweeping as an act of worship etc. God warns *"Do not turn to mediums or necromancers; do not seek them out, and so make yourselves unclean by* them: I am the LORD your God." (Leviticus 19:31 ESV)

Superstition: Belief or way of behaving based on fear of the unknown and faith in magic or luck, that certain things like good luck charms or events will bring good or bad luck. God warns in *1 Timothy 4:7*, *"Have nothing to do with irreverent, silly myths. Rather train yourself for godliness..." (ESV)* If you have dabbled in occult practices and have never renounced your activity, I recommend that you repent, openly denounce, renounce, and break your involvement with occult things by following these steps.

It's important to openly denounce (say out loud) and pray out loud. You can't just repent or say, I'm sorry. You have to break the covenant contract by denouncing (saying out loud) letting Satan and his demons know that you are no longer in the agreement with them.

Family Strongholds

Looking at the state of the family structure today we can see Satan is set on destroying families. The number of people who have a father in the home these days is low. Many people have physical and emotional scars from childhood that have carried over into adulthood and into their own families. No matter how hard we try to deny it or even avoid it, much of our behavior and thinking comes from family influence and the environment we were raised in. Children tend to act out many of the same patterns of behavior that their parents engaged in.

Most people have heard of generational curses. If you haven't, a generational curse is one that is said to be transmitted from one generation to another as a result of disobedience to God. For instance, if there are traits of alcoholism, drug addiction, anger, divorce, incest, poverty, or other ungodly patterns in your family line, it might be said that a generational curse is the reason that you struggle with the same issue. Many Christians are taught they are cursed due to their ancestors' words or deeds, and they live in constant worry that they are being punished for what their ancestors or parents did. They believe they must atone on behalf of their parents and ancestors. This mindset can cause their prayer life, if they have one, to be focused on guilt and shame because they have not truly accepted the truth that Jesus Christ has set us free from the sins of our past and from the sins within our family history.

My family has been plagued with the generational sins of addiction, anger, rejection, fornication, adultery, hatred, incest, molestation, unforgiveness, and more on both sides. You may have been raised believing that sexual sins and children born out of wedlock were common if those before you did it. If one of your parents struggled with anger, you may find yourself experiencing outbursts of rage. The same could be said of worry, greed, pride, and a host of other negative emotions. There can also be physical afflictions like high cholesterol, heart disease, and diabetes from bad eating habits we learned growing up. Some may label these behaviors as generational curses or generational iniquity. I label them not as generational curses but rather as learned behaviors that have developed into a stronghold.

I was a single parent of three children with no help from their fathers. When I made the move from Florida to Georgia I struggled financially for a period. Although I believed in God from a child at this time I was pretty much a babe in Christ. I was always in the prayer line seeking answers and remedy for my struggle. Because of what I believe was genuine concern for me and my children and a lack of understanding, the leaders in my church told me that because of my family background, which I had shared with a few people, I was under a generational curse. I went through deliverance session after deliverance session with no change.

Whatever you're afraid of, it is much more afraid of Jesus than you are of it. Jesus cares about everything that concerns you. Whatever frightens you, take it to Jesus and trust His power to deliver you.

Believing that I was cursed, I spent a lot of time feeling guilty and repenting for things that my ancestors did. I believed that God was punishing me for something that my parents and my grandparents had done. My prayer life was filled with a constant state of fear and worry, complaining, condemnation, guilt, and shame. God was truly trying to break through and set me free, but He could not until I yielded to Him and began to study His Word for myself. Today, I thank God for His mercy, His grace, and His freedom. I cannot stress enough how important it is to get with the Holy Spirit and study the Scriptures for yourself. God says, "If any of you lacks wisdom, let him ask of God, who gives to all liberally and without reproach, and it will be given to him. But let him ask in faith, with no doubting, for he who doubts is like a wave of the sea driven and tossed by the wind" (James 1:5-6).

When Satan works his way into a family, like a domino effect, it increases his chances to trickle his destruction down to future generations if the behaviors and mindsets are not dealt with. This can clearly be seen in the Scriptures. For example, Abraham told lies about his wife (Genesis 12:13). His son Isaac also lied about his wife (Genesis

26:1–11). Jacob, Abraham's grandson lied and stole his brother's birthright, which gained him the name "Jacob the Deceiver" (Genesis 25:19–34).

Jacob's sons and their children also told lies and cheated. Jacob's sons even sold their brother, Joseph, into slavery. The Bible doesn't specifically say each of these men learned their behavior from their father, but can you see how the traits carried on to the next generation?

Another example is in David's family. David was a descendant of a prostitute named Rahab. He committed adultery and murder. David's oldest son, Amnon, raped his half-sister, Tamar, committing incest (2 Samuel 13:11–14). Absalom, his brother, killed Amnon, in revenge for Tamar's rape, and became the eldest son of David. Absalom revolted against his father David and made himself king. When David saw his son gaining power, he fled from Jerusalem with his entire household except for ten concubines.

Absalom later slept with the ten concubines in the sight of all Israel (2 Samuel 16:21–22). Another son of David, Adonijah, died because of a woman (1 Kings 2:17–25). Solomon, the second-born child of David and his wife Bathsheba, despite his wisdom and wealth, was not free from sexual lust. It is said that he had 700 wives. His wives turned his heart to other gods. This led to his downfall. Yet after all this, Mary, Jesus' mother, descended from David's son Nathan, indicating his royal origin.

The stories of these Biblical figures are not there to model perfection but rather to testify to God's mercy in interacting with His flawed creations, which all of us are. Truth is, we're all victims of our ancestor's sin in the Garden of Eden. Everyone is a victim of generational curses because all sin is the effect of the curses laid out by God after Adam's fall. All sin gives the devil footholds and avenues of exploitation in our lives, and everyone falls short of God requirement, thus we have Jesus.

It is clear that our parents' personalities and even their decisions have a significant impact on us. But will God really punish us for something our parents did? God says in Ezekiel 18:20,

"The soul that sins, it [is the one that] shall die. The son shall not bear and be punished for the iniquity of the father, neither shall the father bear and be punished for the iniquity of the son; the righteousness of the righteous shall be upon him only, and the wickedness of the wicked shall be upon the wicked only." (AMPC)

Under the Old Covenant, you were either cursed or punished for breaking the Law. Under the New Covenant, Christ took on all your penalties for breaking God's Law, thereby fulfilling the Law for you. Christ redeemed us from the curse of the law by becoming a curse for us (Galatians 3:13). The curse of sin is finished.

Yes, demons are real. They do attack us, and they do tend to stick to the same bloodlines or families. Although they want you to believe they can, there are no ifs, ands, or buts about it: demons cannot impose curses. The Cross changed everything! No matter what sin is passed from generation to generation in your family the buck can stop with you! Despite the fact that sin can be learned through the generations, each individual is accountable for their own transgressions against the Lord. We do not have to repeat the sinful patterns of those before us. We can now walk in the freedom and forgiveness we have through Christ. Understand that life patterns are not broken by prayer. You have to deal with the root issue.

For instance, praying I break the curse of diabetes and high blood pressure is of no avail if you are not eating healthy and exercising. You can certainly pray for the healing of diabetes and high blood pressure, but you also need to change your eating habits and exercise. You must lay aside the weight that so easily besets you. If you are lazy and won't work, and won't sow into God's kingdom, you overspend, and are consistently "poor mouthing" praying I break the curse of poverty and lack will not change your situation. You can certainly pray about your finances, but you still need to follow God's guidance on giving and curb your spending habits and sow into the kingdom of God. Remember 2 Corinthians 9:6 which says, *"Whoever sows sparingly will also reap sparingly, and whoever sows generously will also reap generously."*

Remember, a spiritual stronghold is a pattern of wrong thinking built into one's thought life, so it is set up in the mind. So praying a prayer to break a generational curse while you keep thinking and living in the life patterns of your parents is of no avail. If you keep practicing the same sins of your parents, you're going to have the same consequences. You must break the life patterns—those learned behaviors—and stop committing the sin your forefathers committed.

Ezekiel 18:31 says, *"Cast away from you all the transgressions which you have committed, and get yourselves a new heart and a new spirit. For why should you die, O house of Israel?"* Christ came to give you a new heart. When you accepted Jesus as Lord, you were saved, which means you got a new heart and the Holy Spirit and the Word of God to help you break those life patterns. When the temptation comes to continue in the pattern, cast down those thoughts! Use the authority of Jesus' mighty name and the power of His blood! Praise God for victory.

Rejection Stronghold

Rejection is difficult no matter how or who it comes from. If you are praying and standing for salvation for a loved one or friend, they may reject you, lie on you and even try to turn others against you. Keep in mind that you are not dealing with flesh and blood (Ephesians 6:12) or their treatment of you. The real battle is for the person's heart as you fight for them in prayer. We battle for our minds as we bring the lies, opinions, and arguments in line with the knowledge of God and who He says we are.

Truth is Satan know that the prayers of the righteous avails much and he wants to bring you to a place where you stop praying for them. Hebrews 12:15 instructs, *"See to it that no one fails to obtain the grace of God; that no "root of bitterness" springs up and causes trouble, and by it many become defiled."* God created us for relationships. This is why we all long for a place to belong—a place to be valued and accepted. God also made each of us for a specific purpose and designed us with specific skills, gifts, and talents unique to our divine assignment and destiny.

Satan knows that every follower of Jesus has a divine assignment and is important in the Kingdom of God. He knows our full potential can only be reached as we use our gifts for the glory of God and the benefit of others. so he assigns Satanic spirits to hinder us. One of these is the spirit of rejection. He uses the spirit of rejection to deter us, hoping we will draw back from our purpose. This is why, at one time or another, we all experience rejection.

Rejection is an open door to a variety of bondages such as anger, envy, fear, rebellion, jealousy, unforgiveness, and more. As with abuse, it's not so much the rejection that opens us up to unclean spirits as our reaction to it. If the emotional wounds left from rejection are not cleansed and released, they will grow and fester into spiritual wounds. Therefore, forgiving those who have rejected us is a vital step in this process. If we want God's help in this healing process, then forgiveness is not an option.

Satan plants rejection through a variety of ways. Most of the time, it comes from those who are supposed to love and accept us. Rejection is such a malicious spirit that it often begins its attack at conception, while the baby is in the womb, or at birth. There is still a great war over the lives and conception of children. Pharaoh (Satan) is still trying to destroy children.

Research has shown that babies can hear what's being said around them while in the womb. They can hear, sense, and react to emotions such as love and rejection. What the mother experiences and thinks about the child and/or the pregnancy directly affects the child. There are different beliefs about what babies can experience in the womb, but here is a story of what happened with a teen mother's unplanned pregnancy and her child.

True story:

A young girl who got pregnant when she was a teen. When she learned that she was pregnant, she was afraid to tell her mother. When her mother found out, she got so upset that she beat the young girl with a stick, yelling that she was going to beat the child out of her. The young girl decided that she would keep the baby, but she was afraid. Throughout her entire pregnancy, people around her talked about how she would not be able to care for the child and the pain of delivery.

Because of the horror stories she listened to, fear stayed with her throughout the pregnancy. When she was in her 9th month, the baby's aunt, who was also pregnant, delivered her baby through a cesarean section. When the young girl went to the hospital to visit the aunt, she saw how much pain she was in and how swollen she was, and she started trembling in fear.

All those emotions the mother was experiencing, the baby was experiencing too, but no one knew that this was happening. When the young girl's son was born, she was proud and loved him very much. She lived with her mother and her siblings. One of her sisters threw the newborn on the floor, trying to kill him. When her mother asked her daughter why she would do something like that to the baby, she said she didn't want the baby there and she wanted to send him away. Thankfully, the baby wasn't physically harmed, but the seed of rejection that was embedded in the baby while he was in the womb was watered. Again, no one knew this.

There were more instances that happened beyond the young mother's control that served to water that seed of rejection. When the child became a teenager, he became withdrawn from the family, and seemed angry all the time. His mother thought that he was dealing with a lot of emotional pain but didn't know why. She thought maybe he had been molested and was afraid to tell it. She questioned him several times and he said nothing like that had happened. She tried everything she knew to help her son, even counseling, but nothing helped.

When the child became an adult, he became estranged from his family. He literally felt no connection to his siblings and treated his mother as if he hated her and she had no idea why. His middle child endured the same rejection in the womb that his father had endured, and they were never able to really connect with each other. In fact he was estranged from a couple of his children. I continued to question the mother who told me that she never felt like she was wanted by her mother. I could see that a seed of rejection entered both the mother and her baby while they were in the womb. If it is not dealt with it will continue to run through the bloodline.

Most people who were abused and rejected as children have grown up with unresolved emotional wounds. This was the case with me until God began to heal me. Rejection in my life began when I was very young. I'm inclined to believe that it actually started in the womb. Both my parents were addicted to heroin. I wasn't born with an addiction, so my mother's addiction must have come after I was born. When I was around three or four years old, my dad took me from my mom and dropped me off at his mother's house. He and my mom had split up, and I guess he felt his mother could give me a better life. I didn't see my mother again until I was 12 years old.

My dad tried to be a good dad, but addiction always got in the way. Growing up with my grandmother was hard. I don't ever remember receiving any love or affection from her. I always felt unwanted and unloved, as if I was in the way. There were a lot of things going on when I was growing up. Rejection seemed to follow me everywhere I went, damaging my self-worth and my ability to love or trust people.

I wanted to be loved, and I looked for it in places and in people that couldn't give me what I needed. When I finally learned to accept the love of God, things began to change for me. I had to do the work. It took prayer and God's Word to set me free. I cast down and cast out all those unhealthy beliefs that the spirit of rejection had embedded in me. Then I had to meditate on and fill my heart with the truth that God loves and accepts me, and He always has. I had to forgive myself for the mistakes the spirit of rejection caused me to make in raising my children and ask them to forgive me.

God is love, and He loves us beyond anything we can comprehend. That doesn't mean He just tolerates you He loves you, He's interested in you, He's concerned about you, and He cares deeply for you. He never wanted us to feel rejected or abandoned. Sin has corrupted the world we live in so much that we rarely experience things the way God intended for us to experience them. He desires for you to know who you really are, and realize how much He loves, accepts, and appreciates you, so that you can live out the fullness of all God has ordained you to be. No matter what the cause, God wants to deliver you. The opposite of rejection is acceptance. Ephesians 1:6 in the New King James Version says that God has *"made us accepted in the*

Beloved" (NKJV).

How To Destroy The Stronghold Of Rejection

Everyone will experience rejection at some point. Jesus the "stone which the builders rejected" understands rejection (Acts 4:11). He was rejected so that we who were separated from God might have acceptance with the Father. The remedy for our problems is to believe that Jesus bore our rejection so that we might have His acceptance with the Father. Come out of agreement with any lies you have believed about yourself and recognize your true identity in the Lord.

Forgive those who have rejected you. Lay down all bitterness, resentment, hatred, and rebellion. Accept the fact that you are accepted in Christ, that God accepts you. Also, you have to accept yourself. Sometimes this is the hardest thing to do. If you are critical of yourself, stop it. You are God's handiwork, His masterpiece. You are the only you there is of you. Of all the things He created in the universe, He has devoted the most time and care to mankind—to you! Let your healing take place. Meditate on Scriptures on God's acceptance and love for you. Here are a few:

- *Romans 8:28 (ESV): "And we know that for those who love God all things work together for good, for those who are called according to his purpose."*

- *Romans 8:31 (ESV): "What then shall we say to these things? If God is for us, who can be against us?"*
- *Psalm 27:10 (ESV): "For my father and my mother have forsaken me, but the LORD will take me in."*
- *Isaiah 41:10 (ESV): "Fear not, for I am with you; be not dismayed, for I am your God; I will strengthen you, I will help you, I will uphold you with my righteous right hand."*
- *Jeremiah 29:11 (ESV): "For I know the plans I have for you, declares the Lord, plans for welfare and not for evil, to give you a future and a hope."*
- *1 Peter 5:7 (ESV): "Casting all your anxieties on him, because he cares for you."*
- *Romans 5:8-10 (ESV): "But God shows his love for us in that while we were still sinners, Christ died for us. Since, therefore, we have now been justified by his blood, much more shall we be saved by him from the wrath of God. For if while we were enemies we were reconciled to God by the death of his Son, much more, now that we are reconciled, shall we be saved by his life."*

- *Also read Romans 8:31-39.*

Stronghold of Addiction

There are many ways Satan destroys individuals and families. The most diabolical, in my opinion, is addiction. There are many types of addictions, including gambling, work, pornography, food, social media, video games, and even shopping, but the one I want to focus on here is substance abuse: illicit drugs and alcoholism. I could be biased because it was around me nearly every day of my life growing up, and I endured much trauma because so many people around me were caught in its trap. I've seen what it does to people and their families. I've seen it destroy businesses and even ministries.

Illicit drug addiction and alcoholism are another one of Satan's most destructive strongholds against mankind. It really doesn't matter what a person's drug of choice is—whether alcohol, marijuana, heroin, meth, opioids, crack, heroin, pills, or the like—drugs and alcoholism are major gateways for demons to implement their plans and agendas from the pit of hell into people's lives. The snare of drug addiction touches nearly every family in the United States in some way, even members of the body of Christ, and it has been doing so for decades. Ever since I can remember, there has been a so-called war on drugs.

I've seen husbands abandon their families, and mothers leave their young children for days at a time while they chase their next high, even selling their child for a high. This demon is so strong that people give up everything God has blessed them with and everything they've worked to achieve for just one more taste of what they crave. But even more than all that, the addict becomes alienated from the very One who wants to set them free, God. What force on earth could do all of that but a demon?

Drug addiction and alcoholism is no respecter of gender, ethnicity, economic level, or age and many who are addicted don't seem to be aware of it or won't admit it. A few years ago, I talked with a man I worked with who revealed that he occasionally smoked crack cocaine. I was surprised at this news because both he and his wife had high-level jobs.

I expressed my thoughts on how dangerous using crack was, but he was under the impression that he could handle the crack, and said he was not addicted. I told him I've known a lot of crack addicts, and every one of them was under the impression that they could handle it, but soon found out that the drug was handling them. He disagreed and defended the drug. He was deceived. He ended up losing everything. I tell you sin will take you farther than you want to go, keep you longer than you want to stay, and cost you more than you want to pay.

Heal me, O Lord, and I shall be healed; save me, and I shall be saved: for thou art my praise. — Jeremiah 17:14

All addictions begin with deception. All addiction begins with deception. When a person does not reject or cast down the lie they give way to temptation. All temptation is rooted in deception. Some people have convinced themselves that since the Bible doesn't say anything against addiction or drugs or alcohol, using them is not so bad. This is deception.

Paul said in 1 Corinthians 6:12, *"All things are lawful unto me, but all things are not expedient: all things are lawful for me, but I will not be brought under the power of any."* Paul was addressing several specific sins the Corinthian believers were tolerating. Some brethren were taking advantage of each other in court, and others were practicing immorality. In this verse, Paul was talking to those who want to justify their sin in the name of their liberty in Christ, but he is letting them know that liberty has limitations. No amount of liberty excuses habitual sin.

The devil lures a person into an addiction with the lie that the reward is greater than the cost. The Bible does speak about addictions – it calls them the lusts of the flesh. What is lust of the flesh? Lust is an intense desire for something or someone or circumstance (e.g., power, money, sex, etc.). Lust of the flesh speaks of any wicked desires stirred by our physical or emotional needs, particularly the desire for pleasures.

"16 For all that is in the world—the lust of the flesh, the lust of the eyes, and the pride of life—is not of the Father but is of the world. 17 And the world is passing away, and the lust of it; but he who does the will of God abides forever." — 1 John 2:16-17

People can reason, twist, and defend their actions and try to convince themselves and others that drugs like marijuana, cocaine, and even heroin are not so bad because they come from plants. Some will even quote Genesis 1:29, where God said, "See, I have given you every herb that yields seed which is on the face of all the earth, and every tree whose fruit yields seed; to you it shall be for food." But just because something grows on the earth and has pretty flowers and green leaves does not mean it was not created by God for the purpose it is used for today. The Bible says:

"Wine is a mocker, strong drink is raging: and whosoever is deceived thereby is not wise" —

Proverbs 20:1 KJV.

Most people who struggle with addiction are loving, caring people who made choices that led them into the destructive behaviors of addiction. The crack addict didn't take their first hit with the intention of becoming addicted. The alcoholic didn't take their first drink intending to become addicted. They may have only been trying to fit in, have some fun, relax, or find relief from some type of trauma, pain, or difficulty in life. They had no intention of the drug controlling them and destroying their lives, but Satan did.

They are people who didn't realize how they were being used by Satan to destroy their own lives. They got into something they no longer have control over. They didn't realize that drugs and alcohol do not offer what they were looking for, but only bring more problems in the end.

No matter how a person gets trapped, God wants to set them free, not just cope with or manage the addiction. I applaud the efforts of secular treatment programs, but the fact is very few are successful over the long haul. I've seen people go in and out of treatment centers, only to come out and go right back to the same thing. They keep going back because there is a real desire to get free, but their hope is in human efforts, not the One who can truly set them free. Rehab treats the problem. God treats the person and the problem. God wants to set them free, not just cope with or manage the addiction, which is what many treatment centers do.

On the other hand, I've seen people go through deliverance and go back to the same thing. I've seen God deliver people completely from all types of addictions, and they never go back. Again, I may be biased, but I am partial to God's way of deliverance. Substance abuse is partly demonic, which means it is partly sin nature, partly spiritual, and partly physiological.

If the treatment or deliverance does not deal with all three, then more than likely the person will continue going around in circles trying to get free. The power of God can deal with all three through a personal relationship with Jesus Christ and the power of the Holy Spirit, which will lead a person and guide them to total freedom from addiction. He will use Christian counselors and Christian rehab facilities when necessary.

Satan is a spiritual being, and his tactic is warfare. He is not going to just sit back and set you free. His ultimate goal is to kill your body and then destroy your soul in hell forever. Even though he may allow you to be "free" for a while, he will never let you be totally free. He will always keep a foothold so he can come in when he needs to. That's why part of their 12-step plan says that you will always be an addict in recovery. The Word of God says in John 8:36, He whom the Lord sets free is indeed!

Satan likes to stay hidden. Sin strives to have a person by himself. It hides out in darkness and shuns the light. It doesn't want to come around people who walk in the light of Christ, for then it will be exposed, so it keeps its victims isolated. The more isolated a person is, the more destructive sin's power is over him. If you want to be free, sin must be acknowledged and brought into the light. Even though God knows all about it, He wants us to humble ourselves and ask Him for forgiveness. We must bring all our sins to God in prayer. Prayer and the Word of God are the most powerful tools we have when it comes to fighting addiction.

He whom the Lord sets free is free indeed! God can heal and deliver a person in an instant, and they will never touch drugs or alcohol again, but that's not always the case. Deliverance from any bondage, including addiction, is usually a process.

It was a process getting into the bondage, and it is often a process getting out because God deals with the whole person, not just the problem. Deliverance from addiction comes in several ways. We cannot try to fit God into our little boxes. Those God sets free typically don't go back. He whom the Lord sets free is truly free indeed. Christ took

ALL our infirmities and afflictions to the cross, including addictions.

> *"4 Surely He hath borne our griefs and carried our sorrows; yet we did esteem Him stricken, smitten of God, and afflicted. 5 But He was wounded for our transgressions; He was bruised for our iniquities. The chastisement of our peace was upon Him, and with His stripes we are healed." — Isaiah 53:4-5.*

> *"No temptation has overtaken you that is not common to man. God is faithful, and He will not let you be tempted beyond your ability, but with temptation He will also provide a way of escape, that you may be able to endure it." — 1 Corinthians 10:13*

If a person is going to get free and stay free, the deceptions they have believed must be broken. If a person doesn't think they have a problem or need help, they won't seek it. Remember, unless the soul yields its rule to the spirit, the spirit cannot rule. Bondage is about something lording over you. If you are your own lord, the bondage has already defeated you and will keep you under its control; but if you surrender that lordship to Jesus the One who is greater than all, then every other lord will have to flee.

Most of the time, it is not until the consequences of the addiction expose the lies that the person realizes what the addiction has done and genuinely cries, "Father, I need help. I want out of this." The story of the prodigal son in Luke 15:11–32 is a good example of this. One day, the prodigal son finally came to himself and realized the insanity of his behavior and all that he had lost. He said, *"I will arise and go to my father, and I will say to him, "Father, I have sinned against heaven and before you..."* (Luke 15:18).

As much as the father loved his son and knew that his decision was a bad one, he did not chase after him, trying to convince him to come back home. He knew that if the son did not see the foolishness of his behavior and came home, it would only be a temporary fix. As a parent I know that waiting on your adult child or teenager to come to their senses can be hard. The father waited until the son felt the impact and consequences of his recklessness. He waited for the son to come to repentance. Because he loved his son, I'm sure he also prayed that he would come to his senses. Any good parent would!

Notice also that the prodigal son humbled himself. He came to his father asking for help. Pride is a major barrier to deliverance. *"God resists the proud but gives grace to the humble"* (1 Peter 5:5). God's power to heal, save, and deliver knows no bounds. no matter who you are, or how long you have been addicted, God can deliver you. Attending church and prayer is essential to breaking free and staying free.

Don't allow the lie that all churches are bad and full of hypocrites to keep you out of church. You need fellowship with other believers. Understand that the Church is not for perfect people who don't think they need help. It is for those who know they need saving from themselves and want to grow in Christ. Many there have walked through what you are dealing with, and can help you get free.

Focus on the answer, not the problem. Jesus Christ is the answer. Through Bible study, prayer, and interactions with other Christians, someone seeking freedom can learn how to live in the freedom Christ has given us. This is one of the reasons a good Bible believing church is important. When the Bible talks about people who shun the Church, it speaks of them as if they are also shunning Christ. Look at what the Word says in Hebrews:

> "[23] *Let us hold fast the confession of our hope without wavering, for he who promised is faithful.* [24] *And let us consider how to stir up one another to love and good works,* [25] *not neglecting to meet together, as is the habit of some, but encouraging one another, and all the more as you see the Day drawing near.*

26 For if we go on sinning deliberately after receiving the knowledge of the truth, there no longer remains a sacrifice for sins, 27 but a fearful expectation of judgment, and a fury of fire that will consume the adversaries. 28 Anyone who has set aside the law of Moses dies without mercy on the evidence of two or three witnesses.

29 How much worse punishment, do you think, will be deserved by the one who has trampled underfoot the Son of God, and has profaned the blood of the covenant by which he was sanctified, and has outraged the Spirit of grace? 30 For we know him who said, "Vengeance is mine; I will repay." And again, "The Lord will judge his people." 31 It is a fearful thing to fall into the hands of the living God.."— Hebrews 10:23-31

God called King David was a man after God's own heart, but David fell into sexual sin with Bathsheba. When God called him on it, David prayed and asked for forgiveness:

"1 Have mercy on me, O God, because of your unfailing love. Because of your great compassion, blot out the stain of my sins. 2 Wash me clean from my guilt. Purify me from my sin. 3 For I recognize my

> *rebellion; it haunts me day and night. 4 Against you, and you alone, have I sinned; I have done what is evil in your sight. You will be proved right in what you say, and your judgment against me is just. 5 For I was born a sinner—yes, from the moment my mother conceived me. 6 But you desire honesty from the womb, teaching me wisdom even there. 7 Purify me from my sins, and I will be clean; wash me, and I will be whiter than snow." (Psalm 51:1-7 NLT).*

It is God's will for you to be healthy and whole. If you are not, the healing promises of God are available to you give you hope. Use them as weapons of war to battle addiction. Believe that God wants to deliver you and that He can deliver you. Even if you are not the addict, but you know and love someone who is, God can deliver them, heal them, and set them free through your prayers. Trust God to hear your prayers. Believe despite what others have said, or the lies Satan tells you God loves you and He loves them. God's heart breaks over your pain and theirs. He is there waiting on surrender so He can deliver you or them from addiction. Isaiah 53:5 says:

> *"But He was wounded for our transgressions, He was bruised for our iniquities; the chastisement for our peace was upon Him, and by His stripes we are healed."*

Remember, *"... the Lord's hand is not shortened, that it cannot save; nor His ear heavy, that it cannot hear"* (Isaiah 59:1).

Here is a sample prayer to give you an idea of how you can pray for yourself and for someone else to break the power of addiction:

Prayer to Break Free from Drugs

Father God, I ask for a hedge of protection around myself, my home, and my family. I plead the blood of Jesus over me and my family. Father, let your healing hand rest over my heart. Jesus came to set the captives free and to release them from darkness. Heal me, O Lord, and I will be healed; save me, and I will be saved, for you are the one I praise. Remove the desire for drugs and alcohol. Let it be demolished now in the name of Jesus. Destroy the blinders and deception that brought about this demonic spirit. I declare in the name of Jesus that I am free from this bondage. I pray that Your Holy Spirit will work in my heart and in my family's hearts, and that Your name will be uplifted and glorified in this situation. In Jesus' name, we pray, Amen.

Prayer For Someone Addicted to Drugs

Heavenly Father, I plead the blood of Jesus and ask

for a hedge of protection around myself, my home, my family, and _____. I plead the blood of Jesus over _____. Let your healing hand rest over _____'s heart. Your word promises to set the captives free and to release them from darkness. I plead the blood of Jesus over _____'s desire for drugs/alcohol. Let the desire be demolished now in the name of Jesus. Destroy the blinders and deception that brought this demonic spirit. I declare in the name of Jesus that _____ is set free from this bondage. I pray that Your Holy Spirit will work in our hearts and in _____, that Your name would be uplifted and glorified in this situation. In Jesus' name we pray, Amen.

Trust the Lord. Believe that He is with you, and nothing can separate you from Him. Remain steadfast in Christ as you walk in faith and victory.

Remember, no matter how much you relapse and struggle, He still loves you and always will. Do not allow guilt to keep you from accepting the help that is offered to you. If you feel like you need more help, talk to a pastor, or seek out a Christian treatment center for your addiction. There are many programs that can meet your needs.

If you don't see results right away, do not become

disheartened and stop praying and believing. In Daniel 10:13, we read that an angel coming to Daniel's aid was detained in battle for 21 days. Our prayers are heard and are effective, but the battle must still be fought.

Stronghold of Fear

Fear is a stronghold that can incapacitate a person and spread panic and despair like a plague in a person's life. It is one of Satan's primary devices to keep people oppressed and trapped. Satan, the father of lies, wants you to speculate about disasters in your future. Understand that God has not given you a spirit of fear but that of power, and of love, and of a sound mind. When you consent to fear, you dwell on a reality that violates God's assignment for your life. In life, there will be trials and adversities we will have to face. We must remember that we have a faithful God who will walk with us through each one of them.

> *"Even though I walk through the darkest valley, I will fear no evil, for you are with me; your rod and your staff, they comfort me.* [5] *You prepare a table before me in the presence of my enemies. You anoint my head with oil; my cup overflows.* [6] *Surely your goodness and love will follow me all the days of my life, and I will dwell in the house of the Lord forever." –Psalm 23:4-6*

Angeline L. Williams

There Shall Be No Negotiations

Pharaoh, like Satan, was opposed to the children of Israel leaving Egyptian bondage to serve God, but Moses left no room for negotiation with Pharaoh. Satan is opposed to unsaved people learning the truth of the gospel and receiving it and he doesn't want saved people to remain saved. So he does everything he can to keep the unsaved bound in his lies and he harasses and creates snares to catch Believers in his web of destruction. When we look closely, we can see obvious similarities between this pharaoh's proposals and how the devil operates.

The devil is a very devious compromiser. He works tirelessly to get us to compromise God's truth. He did it with Moses when he was called to lead the nation of Israel out of Egypt's bondage (Exodus chapters 8–10). Moses delivered what God said: *"Let my people go that they may hold a feast unto me in the wilderness"* (Exodus 5:2). When it became clear that Moses was serious and was not going to give up, Pharaoh (Satan) tried to negotiate with him. His first attempt came after the plagues of turning the water into blood, frogs, lice, and flies. Because these temptations and compromises Pharaoh (Satan) offered

Moses are basically the same compromises Satan offers to God's people today, we can learn a great deal by taking a close look at them.

Notice that the command *"Let My people go that they may serve Me"* is direct, authoritative, and forceful. God wanted His people to be completely delivered from Egypt (sin and bondage) and separated unto Himself. This is what God wants for you and those in your circle today. Their complete freedom from the land of death and darkness is the only thing that He desires, thus He sent His Son. You have been given the authority and strength of Jesus Christ to carry out the purposes of God in advancing His Kingdom, healing the sick, and defeating the works of Satan and the powers of darkness. God has not given you a spirit of fear (2 Timothy 1:7), so if fear comes, cast it down immediately.

Satan is God's enemy. when the enemy comes against you, your family and those in your circle. Be bold and of good courage. God is with you. Jesus Christ will back you up. Pray from your position of authority and boldly declare *"Satan, let _____ go that they may serve God."*

"Go, sacrifice, but stay within Egypt."

"25 Then Pharaoh called Moses and Aaron and said, "Go, sacrifice to your God within the land." 26 But

Moses said, "It would not be right to do so, for the offerings we shall sacrifice to the Lord our God are an abomination to the Egyptians. If we sacrifice offerings abominable to the Egyptians before their eyes, will they not stone us? 27 We must go three days' journey into the wilderness and sacrifice to the Lord our God as he tells us." —Exodus 8:25-27

Like Satan, this pharaoh could not be trusted. The land was under Pharaoh's control, so if Israel had attempted to offer sacrifices to God there, they would have incurred the Egyptian death penalty. We should never compromise on what God has commanded. God had instructed them to travel three days into the wilderness. Israel could not please Egypt and God at the same time, and neither can we.

Pharaoh (Satan) doesn't care if you attend church, just don't attend a Bible-believing church whose goal is to help you learn and grow in Christ. "It don't take all that," he might say. Just dress up, show up, and do your churchly duty. Choose a church with a great choir where the preacher puts on a good show." You can straddle the fence so to speak. You must forsake Egypt. The older generation of Israelites never made it to the Promised Land because they didn't want to forsake Egypt. Jesus taught, *"No man* can serve two masters: for either he will hate the one, and love the other; or else he will hold to the one, and despise the other. Ye cannot serve God and mammon"* (Matthew 6).

Pharaoh (Satan) doesn't have any new tricks. When Satan cannot crush or curse you, he seeks to corrupt you through compromise. Revelation chapter 2 talks about the church at Pergamos, known as the Compromising Church. Several believers there were being influenced by false teaching. Unaware of the spiritual compromise that was happening among them, some began following the teaching of Balaam, and some were following the teaching of the Nicolaitans.

> *"But I have a few things against you: you have some there who hold the teaching of Balaam, who taught Balak to put a stumbling block before the sons of Israel, so that they might eat food sacrificed to idols and practice sexual immorality."* (Revelation 2:14 ESV)

Balaam was a was a prophet of God who was willing to be paid to prophesy what people wanted to hear. The Nicolaitans taught that a little sin is not so bad, that Christians can compromise their convictions for the sake of popularity, money, sexual gratification, or personal gain.

In Numbers 22, we read that the children of Israel camped in the plains of Moab. Balak, the Moabite king, had seen everything the Israelites did to the Amorites. And when the people of Moab saw how many Israelites there were, they were terrified. Look at how God's enemies were afraid of God's people!

The king of Moab said to the elders of Midian, "This mob will devour everything in sight, like an ox devours grass in the field!" So Balak sent messengers to Balaam saying: *"Look, a people has come from Egypt. They cover the face of the earth and are threatening me! Please come at once, curse this people for me, for they are too mighty for me. Perhaps I shall be able to defeat them and drive them out of the land, for I know that he whom you bless is blessed, and he whom you curse is cursed."* So the elders of Moab and the elders of Midian went with money to pay Balaam, and told him what Balak said (Numbers 22).

So Balaam's lust for money caused him to attempt to prophesy against the people of Israel, but when he went forth, the Holy Spirit came upon him and caused him to foretell the wonderful future of Israel instead. Three times he tried to curse Israel, but God restrained him. When his attempt failed and he did not get paid the large reward, he tried another approach. Since he could not curse Israel, he thought he would entice Israel to curse themselves.

He told King Balak that he could get the Israelites to sin against God by enticing them with sexual immorality and food sacrificed to idols. He conspired with the Midianite and Moabite leaders to use the daughters of the Midianites and Moabites as bait to lure the Israelite men to an idolatrous feast. Balaam's wicked plan succeeded, and the Israelites cursed themselves. The Israelites began to sleep with the daughters of Moab and join in with their sacrifices to their gods, eating and bowing down to their gods. God sent a deadly plague to them, and as a result, 24,000 died (Numbers 25—31). Balaam's teaching encourages idolatry. A servant of God who has greed in his heart is committing idolatry.

The Nicolaitans are mentioned in Revelation 2:6 as a group whose doctrine and deeds Jesus despised and hated. They encouraged their followers to lower their godly standards by convincing them that it was alright to straddle the fence, to have one foot in the world and one in Christianity. They taught that Christians can still participate in worldly activities and indulge in sin. This is spiritual compromise, and much like in Pergamum, this evil is attempting to gain a foothold within our hearts and infiltrate the church.

Those who follow the beliefs of the doctrine of Balaam and the Nicolaitans compromise their convictions for the sake of popularity, money, sexual gratification, or personal gain. Can you see this attitude among many in the Body of Christ today? Sincerely think about it. Is there a point where you are willing to disobey God? Can Satan buy you? Who in your life can get you to compromise God's truth? How important is obedience to God to you? Every Believer must fight their own battles over compromise. James 4:17 says, *"Whoever knows the right thing to do and fails to do it, for him it is sin."*

What seems like an insignificant act of disobedience can have monumental results. A little compromise can lead to big changes in your life. Compromise is a slow process. It doesn't come announcing itself. It comes cloaked in something that looks appealing to you. In Genesis chapter 3, when Eve saw that the fruit of the tree was good for food, pleasing to the eye, and also desirable for gaining wisdom, she took some and ate it.

Every desire of ours is not from God. Some are from our flesh, and some are from Satan. The result of Eve acting on her desire is a prime example of just because something looks good, is desirable, and is available, it does not mean that God wants us to partake of it. The existence of a desire does not mean that it should or will be fulfilled.

Galatians 5:9 warns us that a little leaven leavens the whole lump. Satan convinced Eve that taking of the forbidden fruit was no big deal. He convinced her that God was keeping something from her that would improve her life—even make her a god! Her disobedience led to sin in the whole world. Again, Satan has no new tricks. He often frames compromise as "progress." The Holy Spirit will not have us ignorant of Satan's devices and tricks. He will warn us when we are headed for trouble. So it would be wise to listen to and act on what He says when He is warning us of danger.

"Only ye shall not go very far away."

> "So Pharaoh said, "I will let you go, that you may sacrifice to the Lord your God in the wilderness; only you shall not go very far away. Intercede for me." —Exodus 8:28

Okay, you can go, but just don't go too far. This compromise would allow him to maintain control of Israel. The problem is that this would have defeated the purpose of God, which was to bring Israel entirely out of Egypt. Satan loses the primary battle when a person becomes a Christian. He continues the warfare, but the primary battle has been won, so he seeks to persuade the child of God to "stay in the land" and just be a borderline Christian.

We cannot straddle the fence, with God on one side and the world on the other. Ninety-nine and a half won't do. In Mark 4:1-9, Jesus told a parable of a sower and a planter planting seeds. Only a few of the seeds took root and grew. Birds ate some, and some landed on rocky ground. Some were choked out by the cares, riches, and pleasures of life and brought no fruit to maturity. This is the state that Pharaoh and Satan would rather you be in if they can't keep you from being saved.

Philippians 4:6-7 warns,

"6 Be anxious for nothing, but in everything, by prayer and supplication, with thanksgiving, let your requests be made known to God; 7 and the peace of God, which surpasses all understanding, will guard your hearts and minds through Christ Jesus."

Jesus said in John 16:33:

"These things I have spoken to you, that in Me you may have peace. In the world you will have tribulation; but be of good cheer, I have overcome the world."

Moses again steadfastly refused to compromise, and so must we.

"7 Then Pharaoh's servants said to him, "How long

shall this man be a snare to us? Let the men go, that they may serve the Lord their God. Do you not yet understand that Egypt is ruined?" ⁸ So Moses and Aaron were brought back to Pharaoh. And he said to them, Go, serve the Lord your God. But which ones are to go?" (Exodus 10:7-8)

Pharaoh would not listen to God, and he would not listen to common sense. Pharaoh's servants tried to talk some sense into him, but his pride still wouldn't let him relinquish control. So when Moses and Aaron came back, he basically said, let's talk about this some more. Who are those who will go?

"Go you who are men."

"⁸ So Moses and Aaron were brought again to Pharaoh, and he said to them, "Go, serve the Lord your God. Who are the ones that are going?" ⁹ And Moses said, "We will go with our young and our old; with our sons and our daughters, with our flocks and our herds we will go, for we must hold a feast to the Lord." ¹⁰ Then he said to them, "The Lord had better be with you when I let you and your little ones go! Beware, for evil is ahead of you. 11 Not so! Go now, you who are men, and serve the Lord, for that is what you desired." And they were driven out from Pharaoh's presence. — Exodus 10:8-11

Basically, Pharaoh was saying that women and children were not important in the worship of God. And he knew that the men who left their families in Egypt would not go too far or remain away too long. Neither one of those ideas would work because the instructions were for all of Israel to go, regardless of age or gender. Not even the animals were exempt from God's command. God says to you today, "For the promise is to you and to your children, and to all who are afar off, as many as the Lord our God will call." (Acts 2:39). God does not compromise with man, so Moses declined Pharaoh's offer.

Satan will try to convince you to talk about the young boys and girls in the community who are being groomed to sell and use drugs rather than praying for them and declaring Thus says the LORD: "Let My people go, that they may serve Me" to the spirit that is trying to destroy their destiny. The pharaoh said if you want to go, fine, but leave the women.

Satan has worked tirelessly to tear down their self-esteem. He wants you to leave the single mothers who are struggling to raise their children. He's put in a lot of effort to steal their peace and cause them to doubt every good thing in their lives. He wants you to save yourselves, but leave your loved ones behind. "I'll take care of them," he says. But we should never be comfortable leaving our loved ones in Egypt. God sees behind enemy lines. He sees and He knows the strategies Satan is using against us. He wants to give you a strategy to use to stop Satan in his tracks. He wants you to declare to Satan: *"Thus says the LORD: Let My people go, that they may serve Me."*

"Go, only let your flocks and herds stay."

> *"24 Finally, Pharaoh called for Moses. "Go and worship the Lord," he said. "But leave your flocks and herds here. You may even take your little ones with you." 25 "No," Moses said, "you must provide us with animals for sacrifices and burnt offerings to the Lord our God. 26 All our livestock must go with us, too; not a hoof can be left behind. We must choose our sacrifices for the Lord our God from among these animals. And we won't know how we are to worship the Lord until we get there." — Exodus 10:24*

So the pharaoh agrees to let Israel leave and worship God, but he insists that they leave their flocks and herds behind. The people needed the flocks and herds to make sacrifices, so Moses refused this offer. Satan doesn't mind you going to church, but he tries to convince you that there is no need to be sold out in order to please God. He will use distractions, entertainment, watered-down messages, and people to distract you from getting all God wants you to get. He wants to lure God's people into a half-hearted commitment to God, similar to Exodus 10:24.

Jesus said we should be wise as serpents and innocent as doves (Matthew 10:16). Some compromises may appear innocent and necessary on the surface, but God has a reason for saying what He said. Do you agree? God is faithful. Trust Him to bring about all that He intends to do. I encourage you not to give in to that kind of thinking. Trust God and do all that He calls you to do.

Sticking to God's will, Moses replied: *"Our livestock also must go with us; not a hoof shall be left behind, for we must take of them to serve the Lord our God, and we do not know with what we must serve the Lord until we arrive there."*

Not A Hoof Shall Be Left Behind!

Satan is working tirelessly to lead us, our family, and our friends to hell. God wants to save them. Just as God used Moses to deliver the nation of Israel, God wants to use you to deliver your loved ones and those in your circle. God is family-oriented. Family is His design. God is concerned about your whole family and all of your friends, and He wants to use you to save them. Just as Moses led the people out of the land of Egypt, God wants us to lead others out of the land of their bondage by the way He instructs us. The Bible is filled with examples of God saving families. Here are just a few instances:

- God used Noah to save his entire family (Genesis 6:6-13).

- Through Rahab's obedience, her family was spared (Joshua 6:22-27).

- God used Paul and Silas to witness to the Philippian jailer and his entire family believed and was saved (Acts 16:31).

- The Roman centurion named Cornelius prayed, and God sent an angel who said, Cornelius, your daily prayers and neighborly acts have brought you to God's attention. Send for Simon Peter. God used Peter to witness to those gathered in Cornelius' house, and the entire household heard the gospel and were saved (Acts 10:23-45).
- Lydia and her entire family came to Christ (Acts 16:14-15).

God is a covenant keeper. In Genesis chapter 17, God made a covenant with Abraham to bless him and his seed, Abraham's family, throughout their generations (forever). A covenant is a promise, agreement, or contract between two parties. God established a covenant with Abraham so that He could bless you. God covenanted with Abraham and his family, and God has covenanted with you concerning your family. Jesus is our covenant. You part of the covenant is to hold to your faith and expect God to keep His Word to you.

> *"6 "Yet have I set My King upon My holy hill of Zion." 7 "I will declare the decree: The Lord hath said unto Me, 'thou art My Son; this day have I begotten Thee. 8 Ask of Me, and I shall give Thee the heathen for Thine inheritance, and the uttermost parts of the earth for Thy possession."*

"For the promise is to you and to your children, and to all who are afar off, as many as the Lord our God will call." — Acts 2:39

"So they said, "Believe on the Lord Jesus Christ, and you will be saved, you and your household." — Acts 16:31

"For the unbelieving husband is sanctified by the wife, and the unbelieving wife is sanctified by the husband; otherwise your children would be unclean, but now they are holy." — 1 Corinthians 7:14

God is not willing to see any of your family and friends perish. It is His will that all are saved.

"The Lord is not slack concerning his promise, as some men count slackness; but is longsuffering toward us, not willing that any should perish, but that all should come to repentance." — 2 Peter 3:9

You cannot make the decision of salvation for your unsaved family members, friends, and neighbors, but that does not mean there isn't anything you can do. When Moses came before the pharaoh he was told to declare everything God had commanded.

- Ask God to give you a burden for your loved ones and those in your circle.

- Call them by name in prayer, asking specifically for that person's salvation.
- Stand firm on God's promise to seek and save them.
- Live a life that lifts Christ before them rather than repels them from Christ. As you pray and praise God for them to come to Christ, God is listening and setting up situations in their lives so that they can turn to Him.
- Then ask God to send people into their lives to show them His love. No matter how bad they appear to be, they are valuable to God. Don't give up on them.

4 Behold, you fast only to quarrel and to fight and to hit with a wicked fist. Fasting like yours this day will not make your voice to be heard on high. 5 Is such the fast that I choose, a day for a person to humble himself? Is it to bow down his head like a reed, and to spread sackcloth and ashes under him? Will you call this a fast, and a day acceptable to the LORD?

6 "Is not this the fast that I choose: to loose the bonds of wickedness, to undo the straps of the yoke, to let the oppressed go free, and to break every yoke? ⁷ Is it not to share your bread with the hungry and bring the homeless poor into your house; when you see the naked, to cover him, and not to hide yourself from your own flesh? ⁸ Then shall your light break forth like the dawn, and your healing shall spring up speedily; your righteousness shall go before you; the glory of the Lord shall be your rear guard." — Isaiah 58:4-8 ESV

Romans 8:28 tells us that God causes all things to work together for good to those who love God, to those who are called according to His purpose. You have been called according to His purpose. So, when Satan does his dirt, he is serving God's purpose. We just have to stay focused on Jesus and let the Holy Spirit lead us out of whatever Satan brings.

Satan's efforts produced the opposite of what he hoped to achieve in afflicting Jesus, in afflicting Job, and in afflicting you. Satan was instrumental in the betrayal, arrest, torture, and execution of Jesus. But Jesus' death brought about the defeat of Satan (1 Corinthians 2:7-8). With Job, his trials deepened his faith and brought him greater blessings. Satan's efforts against us will accomplish the same thing sooner rather than later if we don't give in to his tactics.

God is looking for people in this last day and hour who are not afraid to confront Satan on behalf of the lost. Not every person who God calls is called to be an apostle, prophet, evangelist, pastor, or teacher. Some people are strategically placed in families to raise godly children and to lead other relatives to Christ. Some are placed in corporate companies to lead co-workers to Christ.

Imagine what would happen if everyone in the Church prayed, "Lord, show Yourself to those who have never heard the Truth of the Gospel. Use us as Your instruments to make this happen." The enemy would tremble because when the Holy Spirit of God moves, he cannot resist.

People are looking for an answer to the problems they face. Most of them don't go to church. You have the answer. People are looking for deliverance and freedom. You are anointed and empowered to help them find it. God is raising up men and women who are giant killers, people who are not afraid of lions dens and fiery furnaces, people who will stand boldly in faith and say with authority, *"Satan, the LORD says let my family go, let my children go, let my friends go, let my coworkers go, let my neighbors go that they may serve the Lord."* God wants people who will stand boldly and speak over marriages and declare, "Satan, the LORD says, let this marriage go, that it may glorify Me."

My point is that God is looking for people who will yield to Him and let Him use them to deliver their families. I believe that if you are reading this book, you are one of those people. You were tailor-made for this. God is calling you, as He did Moses and Aaron, to stand and deliver His Word to the spirits of Satan that are holding people in bondage.

Imagine what would happen if everyone in the Church prayed, "Lord, show Yourself to those who have never heard the Truth of the Gospel. Use us as Your instruments to make this happen." The enemy would tremble because when the Holy Spirit of God moves, he cannot resist.

Angeline L. Williams

Praying In the Spirit

The Bible says, *"The effective, fervent prayer of a righteous man avails much"* (James 5:16). There are many people who believe praying in the Spirit means praying in tongues. The scripture most used to support the idea that praying in the Spirit means praying in tongues is 1 Corinthians 14:13–14, which says, *"13 Therefore let him who speaks in a tongue pray that he may interpret. 14 For if I pray in a tongue, my spirit prays, but my understanding is unfruitful."* Although when we pray in the Spirit, we can pray in tongues, and although praying in tongues can fill a believer's prayer with more power, praying in the Spirit is distinct from praying in tongues.

Two verses that lead me to believe there is a distinct difference: first, Paul says that he is praying with his own spirit. And when I look at Ephesians 6:18, which says Christians are to *"pray always with all prayer and supplication in the Spirit, being watchful to this end with all perseverance and supplication for all the saints."*

If praying in the Spirit is praying in tongues, then how are we to pray with all kinds of prayers and supplications for the saints if no one, including the person praying, understands what is being said? Romans 8:26, which says, *"The Spirit helps us in our weakness. For we do not know what to pray for as we ought, but the Spirit himself intercedes for us with groanings too deep for words,"* suggests one way.

Sometimes we can't find the words to pray, and if we seek Him, the Holy Spirit intercedes for us. The Holy Spirit only speaks and does what the Father says and has said in His Word. This means that the Holy Spirit prompts us to pray the will of God in every situation. Therefore, I encourage you to seek the guidance of the Holy Spirit every time you pray.

Wield Your Sword

Satan has lied over and over and convinced our family, friends, and even us about God and about ourselves. But God's Word is truth. God's Word is alive and active (Hebrew 4:12). This means that it has a vital power inherent to itself. In Matthew chapter 13 Jesus likened the Word of God to a seed. Seed, like the Bible, is alive, and it has the ability to bring forth more life. Hebrews 4:12 also says that God's word is "quick, and powerful, and sharper than any two-edged sword." A two-edged blade cuts in either direction.

In Ephesians 6:17 the Word of God is referred to as

"the sword of the Spirit." The term "word" is taken from the Greek word rhema, which describes something that is spoken clearly in unmistakable terms and undeniable language. In the New Testament, the word rhema carries the idea of a quickened word. An example of a rhema or a quickened word would be as you are praying about a situation, the Holy Spirit brings a Scripture to your mind. You immediately realize that God has given you a verse to stand on and to apply to your circumstances. You've just received a message that was directly spoken by God and dropped into your spirit. That message from God was so keen that it pierced straight through your doubts, intellect, and common sense and took root in your heart.

After you meditated on that Rhema Word from God, it started to release its power inside of you. You began to declare and release out of your mouth what God said to you. The Rhema Word is living and active, so when you spoke it out loud, it went forth, driving back the forces of hell sent against you, your family, your business, your ministry, your finances, your relationship, or your body. Can you recall a time when a particular Scripture sprang up from your innermost being, causing you to feel supercharged and empowered by God's Spirit?

Positive confession and positive affirmation are terms associated with the Law of Attraction concept. Some

Christians believe that speaking, declaring, and confessing God's Word is not biblical. The thing is, every tool or weapon God has given Christians to live in the authority and power we have, Satan has counterfeited. With the new age concept and the Law of Attraction, Satan takes God's Word and twists it to deceive people, just like he did in The Garden with Eve.

The Law of Attraction, manifestation, and New Age are belief systems that teach that the universe responds to our thoughts and words, whether those thoughts and words are negative or positive. What makes this lie so believable is the fact that there are little truths of God's word mixed in, so people compare it to the Scriptures, such as:

- Proverbs 18:21, "Death and life are in the power of the tongue, and those who love it will eat its fruit."

- Joshua 1:8, "This Book of the Law shall not depart from your mouth, but you shall meditate on it day and night, so that you may be careful to do according to all that is written in it. For then you will make your way prosperous, and then you will have good success."

- Mark 11:24, "Therefore I say to you, whatever things you ask when you pray, believe that you receive them, and you will have them."

- Hebrews 11:1, "Now faith is the substance of things hoped for, the evidence of things not seen."

The people who follow this mindset conclude that they are promoting the same things. On the other hand, people believe the lie for the same reason. It is God's Word, the Scriptures, which is alive, active, and sharp, and what drives back the forces of hell sent against you, your family, your business, your ministry, your finances, your relationship, or your body. God's Word spoken in faith and agreeing with God's Word in prayer is about submission and dependence on God. Our words have no real effect. Believing you are wealthy won't make you wealthy. Believing you have the job does not automatically mean it's yours.

Years ago, God spoke to me and said, "Put The Word in Your Mouth." Since then, I have been practicing speaking the Word of God over my life, in my prayers and declaring my faith and I have learned that there is great power in the spoken word. Speaking God's Word can make a huge difference in hiding God's Word in our hearts (Psalm 119:11). When we declare God's Word over us, our family, and friends, we cover ourselves, our home and them in God's truth. This is a biblically sound concept, that Satan doesn't want people to believe and develop.

Look what Apostle John says in Revelation 19:11-16 says,

> "*¹¹ Now I saw heaven opened, and behold, a white horse. And He who sat on him was called Faithful and True, and in righteousness He judges and makes war. ¹² His eyes were like a flame of fire, and on His head were many crowns. He had a name written that no one knew except Himself. ¹³ He was clothed with a robe dipped in blood, and His name is called The Word of God. ¹⁴ And the armies in heaven, clothed in fine linen, white and clean, followed Him on white horses. ¹⁵ Now out of His mouth goes a sharp sword, that with it He should strike the nations. And He Himself will rule them with a rod of iron. He Himself treads the winepress of the fierceness and wrath of Almighty God. ¹⁶ And He has on His robe and on His thigh a name written: KING OF KINGS AND LORD OF LORDS.*"

Notice what verse 15 says: "out of his [Jesus] mouth goes a sharp sword". The Word of God is the Sword that Jesus uses to defeat his enemies. In Matthew 4:4, Jesus used the Word of God to defeat Satan.

In Matthew 17, Jesus stood in authority, spoke, and rebuked the demon, freeing a young boy that the demon had held captive.

In Mark 4, Jesus stood in authority, spoke to the wind and the sea, and calmed the storm that threatened to overtake the boat.

In Matthew 21, when Jesus cursed the fig tree and it withered from the roots, He stood in authority and used words.

In Mark chapter 11, Jesus taught the disciples about mountain moving faith. He told them that whoever says to this mountain, 'Be removed and be cast into the sea,' and does not doubt in his heart, but believes that those things he says will be done, he will have whatever he says.

God's Word is not just the sword of Jesus. It is the sword of every believer. Just as Jesus overcame Satan with God's spoken word, so can every Believer who will believe. When God says to tell Pharaoh, *"Thus says the LORD: Let My people go, that they may serve Me,"* He is saying, stand in your authority and command Satan to let your loved one go. And just like I contended with the pharaoh to set the nation of Israel free, I will contend with those who *contend* with you.

Colossians 2:15 tells us, *"He [Jesus] disarmed the spiritual rulers and authorities [Satan and demons]. He shamed them publicly by His victory over them on the cross."* This means Jesus reduced satanic principalities and powers to nothing—He took away the devil's power to dominate us in any way. So, of course, the devil doesn't want you to believe and use the tools God has given you. He doesn't want you to use your faith. He doesn't want you to pray. He doesn't want you to read and speak the Word of God, and he doesn't want you to attend a Bible believing church that teaches you how to use your tools. It is God's will that we take our position of dominion God intended from the beginning.

God has given us the strategy to deal with the demon powers that want to destroy our family. One of the greatest ways to fight the enemy and stand in the gap for our loved one's freedom is to stand in the authority and power we have in Christ and pray prayers combining Scripture and praise. Through the Spirit of God in you, you have the power to cast Pharaoh (Satan) out of your family members. You have the authority to declare—speak your faith. Don't let up! Be strong and of good courage, and command as God said: "Satan, thus says the LORD: Let _____ go, that they may serve Me."

There are several Bible verses that you can pray and stand on for your family members salvation and deliverance. Here are a few examples to help guide you in your prayers. Where you see _____ go as your person's name.

- For God so loved _____, that he gave his

only Son, that if _____ believes in him, he will not perish but have eternal life. (John 3:16)

- Father God, help _____ to comprehend the breadth, and length, and depth, and height of the love of Christ, and to know this love that surpasses knowledge. (Ephesians 3:18-19)

- Father God, in the name of Jesus I declare that me and my house we will serve the Lord." (Joshua 24:15)

- In the name of Jesus I decree _____ will be kind to others, tenderhearted, forgiving others as God in Christ forgave him. (Ephesians 4:32)

- In the name of Jesus let the inheritance of the Lord come upon my family as it did upon the tribes of Israel (Joshua 13:19).

- Lord I ask You to give _____ the Spirit of wisdom and revelation of Christ, that the eyes of their heart would be opened so that they will know and cherish the hope to which he has called them; the riches of his glorious inheritance in the saints (God's people); and what is the immeasurable greatness of his power in their lives, in accordance with the working of his mighty strength. (Ephesians 1:17-19)

- Father God, I thank You for leading _____ to

repentance and that _____ is turning to You that their sins may be wiped out. (Acts 3:19)

- The Son of Man came to seek and to save _____. (Luke 19:10)

- Father God, thank You that _____ will be saved and come to the knowledge of the truth. (1 Timothy 2:4)

- Father God, I thank You that You are not slow to fulfill Your promise as some count slowness, but patient toward _____, not wishing that _____ should perish, but that _____ should reach repentance. (2 Peter 3:9)

- I declare that God's kindness will lead _____ to repentance. (Romans 2:4)

- In the name of Jesus I decree _____ is free, born-again, spirit-filled, healed, sealed, and delivered. Satan loose _____ back off, and get out in Christ Jesus' Name.

- In the name of Jesus I decree _____ shall submit to God. Resist the devil. (James 4:7)

- Father God, Jesus said that no man can come to Him unless the Father draws them. I ask You to have compassion upon _____. Call them to Jesus. Give them the desire and the Grace to respond and to reach out, that they may have a revelation of Jesus and who He is. Where there is a heart of stone, Father, give _____ a heart of flesh; soften _____'s heart to _____ Lord. Show _____ Your mercy and compassion and make a way out for them, Father. (John 6:44, Ezekiel 36:26)

- Father God, I ask You move upon _____'s heart to accept the Truth of Christ. Give them a heart to know You, that You are the Lord, so that they will be Your people, and You will be their God. May they return to You with all their heart" (Jeremiah 24:7).

- Father God, use me to open _____'s eyes and turn them from darkness to light, and from the power of Satan to God, so that they may receive forgiveness of sins and a place among those who are sanctified by faith in You" (Acts 26:18).

When you declare and pray God's Word over them, you are putting pressure on Satan to release them. You may see the fruit of your prayers immediately, or it may take some time. Like the pharaoh resisted, Satan may resist you and offer compromises, but don't fall for the okey-doke. Stick to God's Word. Keep praying and keep praising God until all are saved. God will do all He can to get your loved ones to respond to His voice. Trust God's plan for your loved ones, especially your adult children who may have gone astray. There is one Scripture that I continue to stand on for my adult children: *"The seed (offspring) of the righteous will be delivered"* (Proverbs 11:21). Remember, one of our greatest weapons is prayer. God specializes in doing the impossible, and He can change even the hardest of hearts.

Scriptures for Battle

As soldiers in the Army of the Lord, we are never to go into battle without our Sword of the Spirit—God's Word. Jesus is our example that, when faced with spiritual attacks from Satan and his minions, we should use God's Word as a weapon against them so that we may win in spiritual warfare. There are many Scriptures you can pray and build your faith. Here are some that will arm you with the sword needed to stand firm during these tumultuous times.

- **Proverbs 21:31**: The horse is prepared for the day of battle, but deliverance is of the Lord.

- **Isaiah 54:17**: No weapon formed against you shall prosper, and every tongue which rises against you in judgment you shall condemn. This is the heritage of the servants of the Lord, and their righteousness is from Me," says the Lord.

- **2 Corinthians 10:4-5**: For the weapons of our warfare are not [a]carnal but mighty in God for pulling down strongholds, casting down arguments and every high thing that exalts itself against the knowledge of God, bringing every thought into captivity to the obedience of Christ,

- **Psalm 18:2**: The Lord is my rock and my fortress and my deliverer; my God, my strength, in whom I will trust; my shield and the horn of my salvation, my stronghold.

- **1 John 4:4**: You are of God, little children, and have overcome them, because He who is in you is greater than he who is in the world.

- **Isaiah 41:10**: Fear not, for I am with you; be not dismayed, for I am your God. I will strengthen you, yes, I will help you, I will uphold you with My righteous right hand.

- **Psalm 20:7**: Some trust in chariots, and some in horses; but we will remember the name of the Lord our God.

- **Ephesians 6:10-13**: Finally, be strong in the Lord and in his mighty power. Put on the full armor of God so that you can take your stand against the devil's schemes. For our struggle is not against flesh and blood, but against the rulers, against the authorities, against the powers of this dark world and against the spiritual forces of evil in the heavenly realms. Therefore take up the whole armor of God, that you may be able to withstand in the evil day, and having done all, to stand firm.

- 2 Corinthians 10:3-5 For though we walk in the flesh, we are not waging war according to the flesh. For the weapons of our warfare are not of the flesh but have divine power to destroy strongholds. We destroy arguments and every lofty opinion raised against the knowledge of God, and take every thought captive to obey Christ...

- James 4:7: Submit yourselves therefore to God. Resist the devil, and he will flee from you.

- 2 Thessalonians 3:3: "But the Lord is faithful. He will establish you and guard you against the evil one."

- 1 Peter 5:8: Be sober-minded; be watchful. Your adversary the devil prowls around like a roaring lion, seeking someone to devour.

- 1 John 5:4-5: For everyone who has been born of God overcomes the world. And this is the victory that has overcome the world—our faith. Who is it that overcomes the world except the one who believes that Jesus is the Son of God?

- 2 Corinthians 10:4: For the weapons of our warfare are not of the flesh but have divine power to destroy strongholds.

- Ephesians 6:11-12: Put on the whole armor of God, that you may be able to stand against the schemes of the devil. For we do not wrestle against flesh and blood, but against the rulers, against the authorities, against the cosmic powers over this present darkness, against the spiritual forces of evil in the heavenly places.

- Matthew 18:18-20: Truly, I say to you, whatever you bind on earth shall be bound in heaven, and whatever you loose on earth shall be loosed in heaven. Again I say to you, if two of you agree on earth about anything they ask, it will be done for them by my Father in heaven. For where two or three are gathered in my name, there am I among them."

- **Ephesians 6:12-18**: ¹² For we do not wrestle against flesh and blood, but against principalities, against powers, against the rulers of the darkness of this age, against spiritual hosts of wickedness in the heavenly places. ¹³ Therefore take up the whole armor of God, that you may be able to withstand in the evil day, and having done all, to stand. ¹⁴ Stand therefore, having girded your waist with truth, having put on the breastplate of righteousness, ¹⁵ and having shod your feet with the preparation of the gospel of peace; ¹⁶ above all, taking the shield of faith with which you will be able to quench all the fiery darts of the wicked one. ¹⁷ And take the helmet of salvation, and the sword of the Spirit, which is the word of God; ¹⁸ praying always with all prayer and supplication in the Spirit, being watchful to this end with all perseverance and supplication for all the saints—

- Isaiah 54:17: No weapon that is fashioned against you shall succeed, and you shall confute every tongue that rises against you in judgment. This is the heritage of the servants of the Lord and their vindication from me, declares the Lord."

- Psalm 84:11: For the Lord God is a sun and shield; the Lord bestows favor and honor. No good thing does he withhold from those who walk uprightly.

- **2 Chronicles 20:15**: And he said, "Listen, all you of Judah and you inhabitants of Jerusalem, and you, King Jehoshaphat! Thus says the Lord to you: 'Do not be afraid nor dismayed because of this great multitude, for the battle is not yours, but God's.

- **Psalm 27:1-3**: [1] The Lord is my light and my salvation; whom shall I fear? The Lord is the strength of my life; Of whom shall I be afraid? [2] When the wicked came against me to eat up my flesh, my enemies and foes, they stumbled and fell. [3] Though an army may encamp against me, my heart shall not fear; Though war may rise against me, in this I will be confident.

- **Isaiah 54:15**: Indeed they shall surely assemble, but not because of Me. Whoever assembles against you shall fall for your sake.

- **Psalms 35:1**: Plead my cause, O Lord, with those who strive with me; fight against those who fight against me.

- **Psalms 144:1**: Blessed be the Lord my Rock, Who trains my hands for war, and my fingers for battle.

- **Romans 8:37**: Yet in all these things we are more than conquerors through Him who loved us.

- **Zechariah 4:6-7**: … "This is the word of the Lord to Zerubbabel: 'Not by might nor by power, but by My Spirit,' says the Lord of hosts. 'Who are you, O great mountain? Before Zerubbabel you shall become a plain! And he shall bring forth the capstone with shouts of "Grace, grace to it!" '

- **2 Timothy 4:18**: And the Lord will deliver me from every evil work and preserve me for His heavenly kingdom. To Him be glory forever and ever. Amen!

- **Psalms 91:1-2**: He who dwells in the secret place of the Most High shall abide under the shadow of the Almighty. I will say of the Lord, "He is my refuge and my fortress; my God, in Him I will trust."

- **Proverbs 18:10**: The name of the Lord is a strong tower; the righteous run to it and are safe.

- **Revelation 12:11**: And they overcame him by the blood of the Lamb and by the word of their testimony, and they did not love their lives to the death.

- **James 4:7**: Therefore submit to God. Resist the devil and he will flee from you.

- **Mark 16:17-18**: ¹⁷ And these signs will follow those who believe: In My name they will cast out demons; they will speak with new tongues; ¹⁸ they will take up serpents; and if they drink anything deadly, it will by no means hurt them; they will lay hands on the sick, and they will recover."

- **Deuteronomy 3:22**: You must not fear them, for the Lord your God Himself fights for you.'

- **1 Corinthians 15:57**: But thanks be to God, who gives us the victory through our Lord Jesus Christ.

- **Habakkuk 3:19**: The Lord God is my strength; He will make my feet like deer's feet, and He will make me walk on my high hills.

- **Matthew 16:18**: And I also say to you that you are Peter, and on this rock I will build My church, and the gates of Hades shall not prevail against it.

- **Jeremiah 1:19**: They will fight against you, but they shall not prevail against you. For I am with you," says the Lord, "to deliver you."

- **Isaiah 40:31**: But those who wait on the Lord shall renew their strength; they shall mount up with wings like eagles, they shall run and not be weary, they shall walk and not faint.

- **Psalm 34:7**: The angel of the Lord encamps all around those who fear Him, and delivers them.

About The Author

Pastor Angeline L. Williams is a native of Florida, presently living in Atlanta, Georgia. She was ordained to preach the gospel by in 1996. God has embedded in Pastor Angeline a passionate love for His Word and a fervent desire to see the lost come to know Jesus Christ and to see the Bride of Christ living to her full potential and capacity, prepared for Christ's return.

She is a bold and transparent preacher whose messages and books are illuminated with revelation and a depth of wisdom and insight resulting from decades of study and relationship with God. She is the owner of Williams DocuPrep, where she provides self-publishing services to Christian and business writers. For more information visit her website at: www.williamsdocuprep.com.

She is available to speak at churches, groups, conferences, workshops, and anywhere God opens a door for her to share what He has given her. To inquire about her availability to speak at your event, visit her website: www.angelinelwilliams.com.

Angeline L. Williams

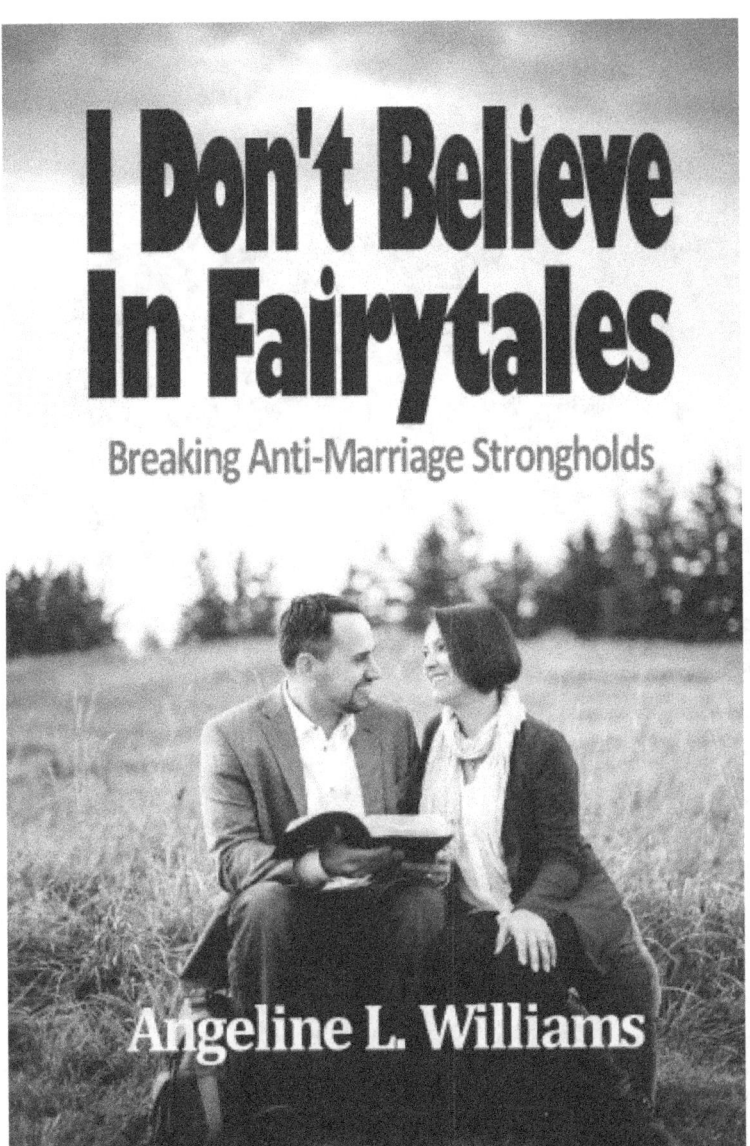

LET MY PEOPLE GO That They May Serve Me!

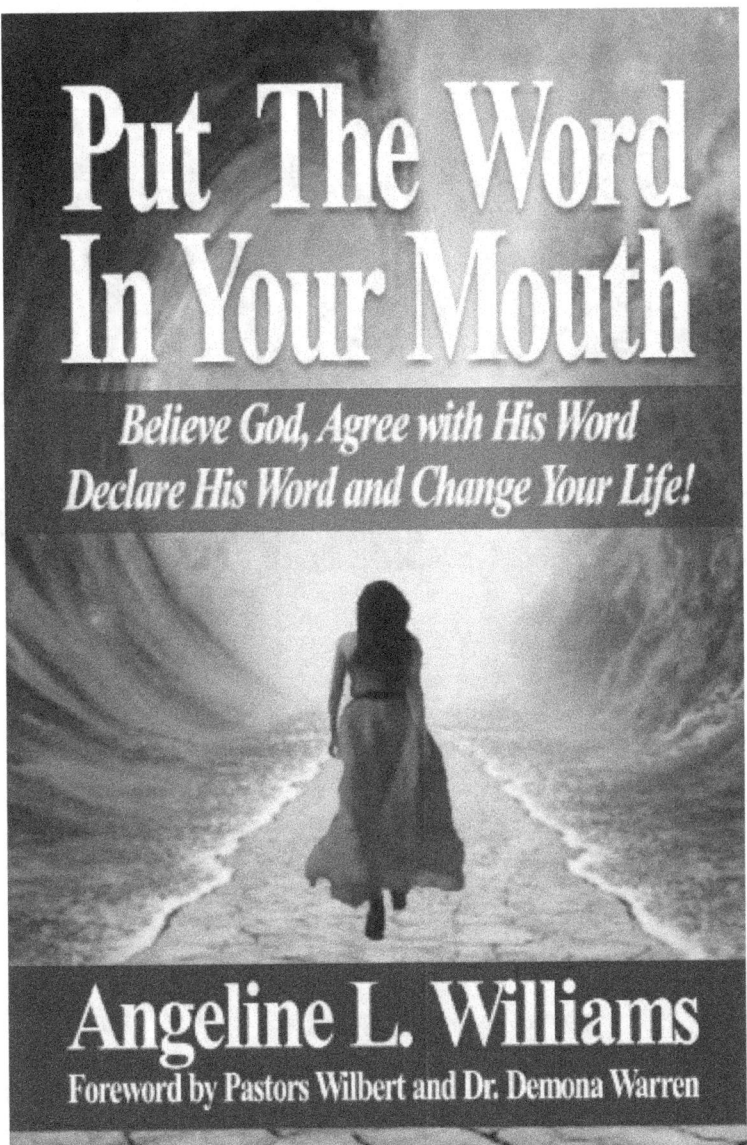

LET MY PEOPLE GO That They May Serve Me!

www.ingramcontent.com/pod-product-compliance
Lightning Source LLC
Chambersburg PA
CBHW072158070526
44585CB00015B/1197